THE LEICESTER AND MELTON MOWBRAY NAVIGATIONS

Dedicated
with an exile's affections
to my native county
of Leicestershire

THE LEICESTER AND MELTON MOWBRAY NAVIGATIONS

Philip A. Stevens

First published in the United Kingdom in 1992 by
Alan Sutton Publishing Ltd · Phoenix Mill · Far Thrupp · Stroud · Gloucestershire
in association with Leicestershire County Council Museums, Arts and Records Service

---

First published in the United States of America in 1992 by
Alan Sutton Publishing Inc · Wolfeboro Falls · NH 03896–0848

British Library Cataloguing in Publication Data

Stevens, Philip
Leicester and Melton Mowbray navigation.
I. Title
386.48094254

ISBN 0-86299-187-0

Library of Congress Cataloging in Publication Data applied for

Typeset in 10/12 Palatino.
Typesetting and origination by
Alan Sutton Publishing Limited.
Printed and bound in Great Britain by
Hartnolls, Bodmin, Cornwall

Contents

List of Illustrations

Preface

Many years ago, when I was a very small boy, I was taken to see a pageant in which the city of Leicester patted itself on the back in the blankest of blank verse at having managed to survive for a very long time. All manner of things and people were dragged in, some of them having rather tenuous connections, others none at all, with the town's history: Wolsey, who came only for the purpose of laying his weary bones there; Charles I, who knocked the place about in a manner more commonly associated with his great rival; even Stephenson's *Rocket* which never came anywhere near Leicester, all were made much of. The whole show took place within a few hundred yards of the Leicester Navigation, which had done so much more for the people of Leicester than any of the glamorous characters prancing about in the pageant: and which was ignored by that Jubilee, just as it was forgotten by the town.

When, many years later, I went to live near Melton Mowbray, I found that the same oblivion had overtaken the Melton Navigation. Our village batsmen crossed the dried-up bed of the navigation on their way between the pavilion and the wicket; but nobody seemed to know that there had ever been a canal there, let alone that it was once a prosperous concern.

Writing this book has been a labour of love, and a moving one, for as my work drew to a close, I left my native county for a West Country exile. By the waters of Parrett and Tone I have sat down – not to weep, but to recall the long days of joyous work in record office, libraries, and in the field, which went into the making of it. If it opens the eyes of some, and especially my fellow Leicestershire men, to what our county owes to these two waterways, I shall have repaid some of what I owe to the shire that made me.

Philip A. Stevens

Acknowledgements

This book has been based as far as was possible on contemporary writings; on the one hand, official records kept by the Leicester Navigation and the other corporate bodies – canal companies, railway companies, and Leicester Town Council chiefly – with which it was involved, and on the other, accounts and opinions set down by outsiders, either in newspapers or in private correspondence. My thanks must first, therefore, be directed to the custodians of these witnesses of history as it was being made. Foremost must come the British Transport Historical Records Office in Porchester Road, London, which, while I was working there, was transformed into a section of the Public Record Office and has since been removed to Kew. Not that it made any difference to the service I received: both before and after that change, the staff gave me every courtesy and assistance, and I am indeed grateful to Mr Fowkes in BR days, and Mr Barlow of the PRO, and their staffs.

Locally, I am indebted to the County Archivist at the Leicestershire County Record Office, and to the Director and Keeper of Archives at Leicestershire Museum, and their staffs for their enthusiastic assistance, which, apart from being helpful, I always found heartening (occasionally, research workers are badly in need of a mental tonic!). The same was true of the staff of the Leicester City Reference Library: without their files of local newspapers and pamphlets, it would have been quite impossible for me to have written the early history of my two navigations, and I acknowledge with pleasure the kindness of the City Librarian and his staff in making these available to me.

The Clerk of the Records and his staff were of the greatest assistance to me in unearthing relevant material from the records of Parliament, especially in connection with the relations of the Melton and the Midland Railway, and I thank them.

Nobody who has done any work on canal history will be surprised to learn that Richard Hutchings, formerly of the Waterways Museum at Stoke Bruerne, overwhelmed me with kindness. One of the busiest of men, he never failed to find time to help, and produced some real gems which have enriched my text.

My fellow members of the Railway and Canal Historical Society have, as always, been generous with help and advice. I would particularly mention Mr P. Stevenson, Mr K. Cheetham, and Mr D.H. Tew. Naturally, I owe much to Mr Tew's book on the Oakham Canal, which played a large part in the history of Melton Navigation.

On looking back, I feel that I owe a debt to the numerous Leicestershire teachers who bombarded me with queries about Leicestershire canals (which I was delighted to receive and, when I could, answer) while I was living among them, and got me to talk to their pupils; in fact the very last thing I did as a member of Leicester Museums' staff was to hold a seminar on the Leicester line for a group of local schoolboys. I think I got to know from these what people want to know about their canals. The same applies to the students at my evening courses, which the courtesy of Leicester University Adult Education Department enabled me to run for many years, and which I miss so much. That I learned more than my students did may emerge from my book.

Charles Hadfield asked me to write this book, and I thank him – not only for his never-failing help, but also for the sheer pleasure writing it has given me.

In bringing the book into the shape it has taken, the advice and help of Michael Handford was invaluable, and I gratefully acknowledge it.

And most of all, I am indebted to my wife, who has been the inspiration of this and of all my work.

Philip A. Stevens, 1974

Sadly, my husband did not live to see the publication of this book, but I am very happy that the results of his many years of research will, at last, see the light of day, through the kind offices of the Leicestershire Museums, Arts & Records Service, where he worked for thirty-four years. My very sincere thanks go to the Director, Tim Schadla-Hall who has done so much to further the project, steering a way through great difficulties; to Geoffrey Bowles for his unstinting work in editing the text, to Peter Stoddart for producing two first-rate maps with all his usual professionalism and attention to detail, to Janette Shepherd for her cheerful help in the LRO selecting illustrations, and finally, to Ruth Kosowicz and Sue Price who have prepared the typescript, nobly coping with all the seemingly trivial and endless details. I am, indeed, grateful.

Valerie Stevens, 1992

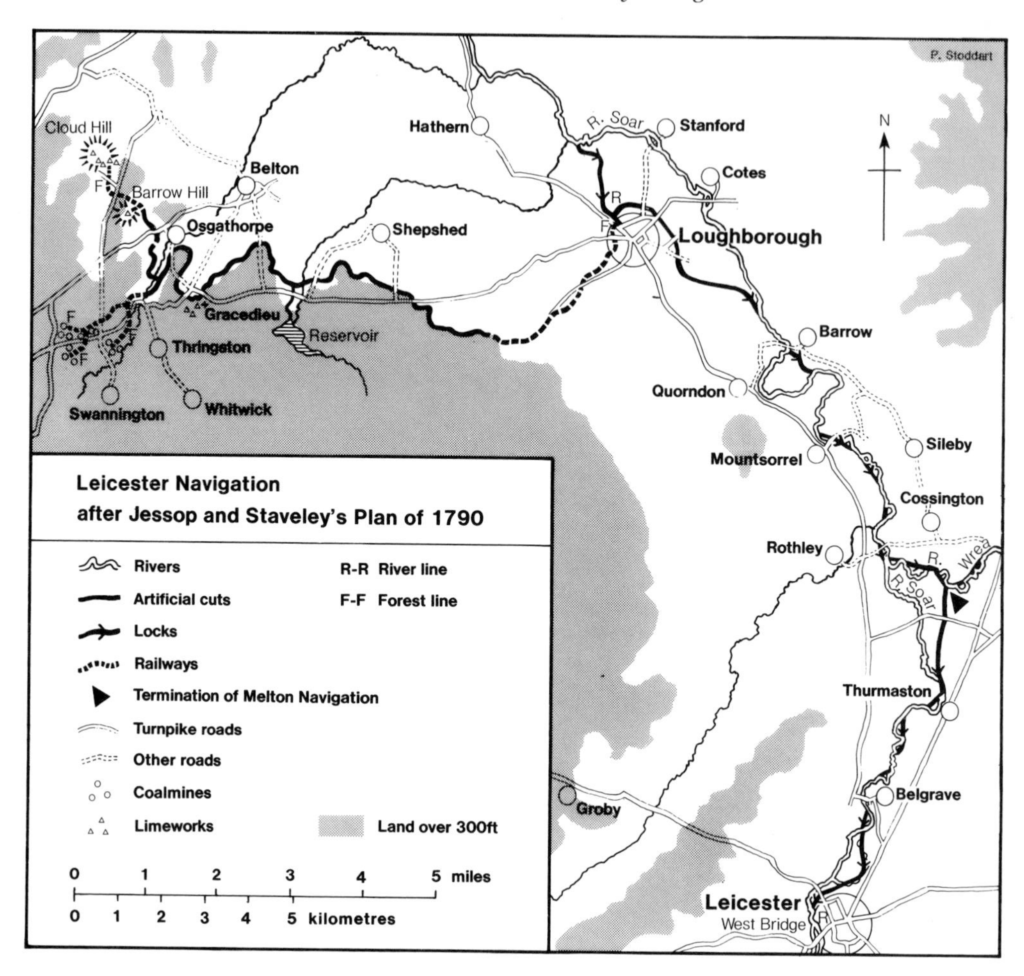
P. Stoddart
N
Cloud Hill
Barrow Hill
Belton
Osgathorpe
Hathern
R. Soar
Stanford
Cotes
Shepshed
Loughborough
Gracedieu
Reservoir
Thringston
Swannington
Whitwick
Barrow
Quorndon
Mountsorrel
Sileby
Cossington
Rothley
R. Wreak
R. Soar
Thurmaston
Belgrave
Groby
Leicester
West Bridge
Leicester Navigation
after Jessop and Staveley's Plan of 1790
Rivers
Artificial cuts
Locks
Railways
Termination of Melton Navigation
Turnpike roads
Other roads
Coalmines
Limeworks
R-R River line
F-F Forest line
Land over 300ft
0 1 2 3 4 5 miles
0 1 2 3 4 5 kilometres

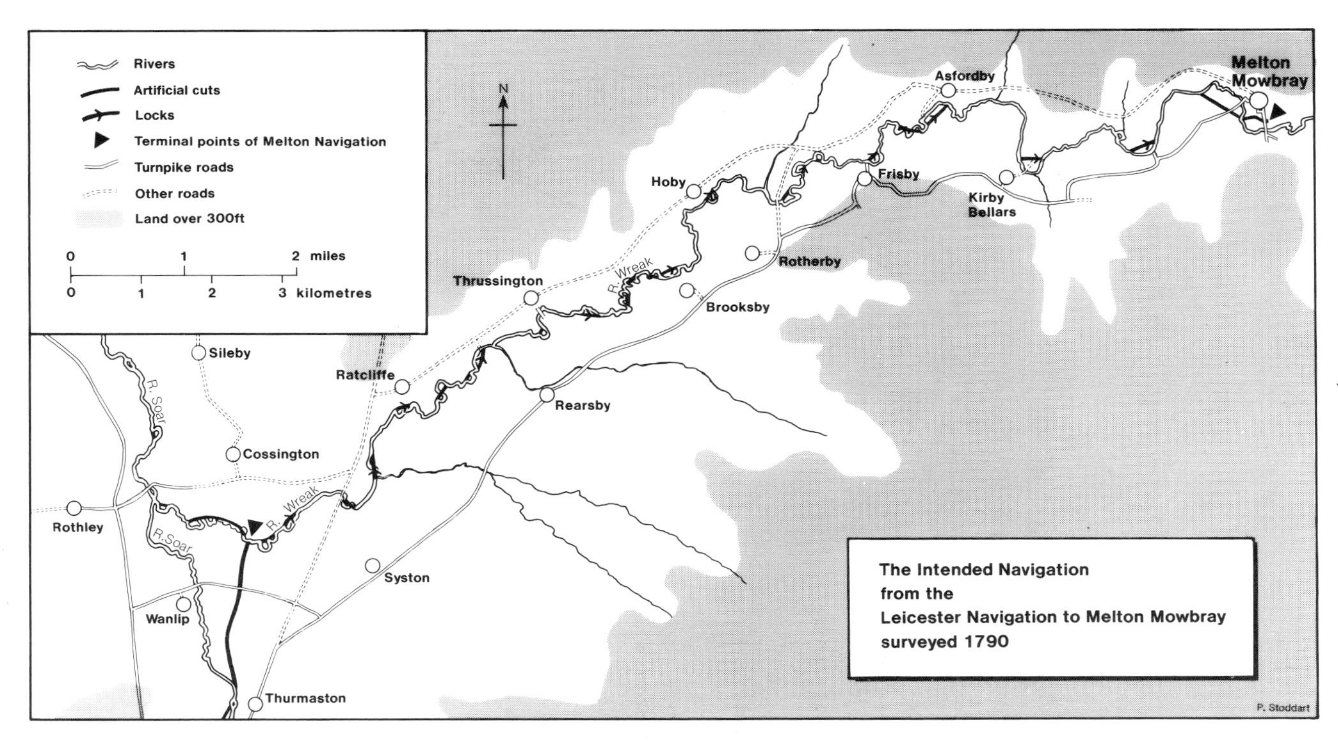
The Intended Navigation
from the
Leicester Navigation to Melton Mowbray
surveyed 1790
Rivers
Artificial cuts
Locks
Terminal points of Melton Navigation
Turnpike roads
Other roads
Land over 300ft
0 1 2 miles
0 1 2 3 kilometres
N
Melton Mowbray
Asfordby
Kirby Bellars
Frisby
Rotherby
Brooksby
Hoby
R. Wreak
Rearsby
Thrussington
Ratcliffe
Syston
Cossington
Sileby
Thurmaston
Wanlip
R. Soar
Rothley
P. Stoddart

Abbreviations

LJ	*Leicester Journal*
LC	*Leicester Chronicle*
LH	*Leicester Herald*
BTHR	British Transport Historical Records (now Public Record Office)
LRO	Leicestershire Record Office

CHAPTER 1
The Leicester Navigation: Early Days

Precursors

In 1778 an event fraught with important consequences for Leicester, and indeed for much of Leicestershire, occurred: the first line of navigable waterway in the county was opened, the first fruits of an intermittent agitation going back at least to the early seventeenth century. True, the waterway was not a spectacular one, being only the canalization of some $9\frac{1}{4}$ miles of the River Soar from its junction with the Trent to the town of Loughborough. But it was important, and became more so with the opening of the Erewash Canal in 1779, for the two navigations between them formed an excellent transport system from the coalmines of the Nottinghamshire–Derbyshire border region to the northern and eastern parts of Leicestershire, a district notoriously lacking in coal. And, more important, higher up the Soar, a mere 15 miles away, lay Leicester, the largest potential market for coal in the county, and a town with problems as regards its coal supply. For the natural source of coal for the county town, the coalfield of west Leicestershire, was separated from it by the wastes of Charnwood Forest, and transport was so difficult that the commonest means of bringing coal to Leicester was by the slow and expensive method of trains of packhorses. There are signs that the output of the pits in the west increased during this period: a new mine was opened at Measham in 1777, and four pits were in full production at Swadlincote in the same year[1] but it is more likely that the output of the former went to the Coventry Canal, and of the latter to the Trent & Mersey Canal, rather than Leicester having the benefit of it.

The new navigation (known as the Soar or, later, Loughborough Navigation) soon attracted the products of the Erewash Valley pits, and by 1780 coal was being offered for sale at Loughborough wharf from West Hallam, Heanor, Eastwood, Denby, Shipley and Ilkeston, at a price averaging 10s. (50p) per ton, the more expensive coals seldom exceeding 11s. (55p). These prices compared favourably with Leicestershire coal.

The recently opened colliery at Heather, for example, was advertising its coal at a pithead price of 9s. (45p) per ton, but land transport to Loughborough would have added greatly to this price. At Staunton Harold, Earl Ferrers had to order a reduction in the price of his coal after the canal opened. A brisk trade in Derbyshire coal grew up at Loughborough wharf, on at least one day no fewer than sixty wagons being loaded there.[2] No doubt much of this coal went to consumers in Loughborough itself or to surrounding villages, but the navigation basin was situated alongside the Derby–Leicester turnpike road, and a growing proportion of the coal found its way to Leicester, where again it competed with Leicestershire coal. So great did the flow become that the turnpike trustees were forced to build a new weighing machine north of Leicester and to impose stringent regulations regarding the weight of vehicles and the width of their wheels, the restrictions being more severe in winter when the road was more susceptible to damage.[3] The attempt does not seem to have been wholly successful, if a comment made some years later in the *Leicester Journal* is to be believed, for it is there stated that on account of the great quantity of coal, lime, and other heavy goods taken along the road, plus recent heavy rains, it was 'ruinous, and almost wholly impassable for carriages'.[4]

Since the Erewash and Loughborough Navigations between them had done so much to reduce the price of coal in the Loughborough area, it was logical that an extension of the line to Leicester itself would bring similar benefits to the townspeople there. This was pointed out by the *Leicester Journal*, which scornfully referred to the 'supineness' of the local people in preferring to spend money on elections rather than on extending navigation to Leicester and up the Soar's chief tributary, the Wreake;[5] and this view was supported by 'A Proprietor of the Erewash Canal', who asserted that coal would thereby be sold in Leicester at 10s. 1d. (50½p) per ton – a reduction of nearly 2s. (10p).[6] But the 'supine' gentlemen of Leicester were not so immersed in elections as the *Journal* believed, for they were in fact already considering such an extension;[7] and on 20 May 1780, the *Journal* carried the first official notice intimating that the project was on foot. Would-be subscribers were asked to leave their names at the *Journal* office. If sufficient interest were shown, the subscribers would be called on to pay 1 per cent of their shares to cover a survey and estimate, and a General Meeting summoned.[8] Immediately afterwards, a General Meeting was called at the Exchange in Leicester. The promoters had evidently decided to reverse their original programme, for one of the purposes of this meeting was to choose a surveyor and draw up his instructions.[9] A committee was to be elected, a clerk appointed, and those present were to be requested to pay a percentage of their subscriptions, though the amount they were to be asked for was left blank!

The meeting was duly held on 12 June 1780, not at the Exchange but at the town's chief civic building, the Guildhall; this surely indicated official support from the corporation. The surveyor's instructions were drawn up in some detail. He was to examine the district for the best line for a navigation; if there were several equally good, he was to list them all, with their respective merits and defects, especially as regards the traffic they could carry and the cost of their construction and upkeep. He was then to prepare an estimate for making and also maintaining all of them, especially the cheapest, including everything down to the cost of the Act. Finally – a requirement which would scare many potential surveyors off – he was to say how accurate his estimate was likely to be! Whoever drew up these exacting requirements worked very conscientiously, and the promoters were rewarded by securing the services of as able an engineer as England could show at this period: William Jessop, then in the early stages of a most distinguished career. A committee of five was set up to get matters moving, the proposed 1 per cent call on capital was made, and a further meeting was arranged for 17 July.[10] This, meeting, however, was never held. It was postponed to 28 August, then postponed again to a date to be announced in due course.

And that was the last to be heard of this project, the intended line of navigation between Loughborough and Leicester relapsing into obscurity, at least as far as the records go, for several years. But in the controversy about it which briefly sprang up following the announcement of the June meeting, a letter from 'A Friend to the Public' appeared in the *Journal* on 27 May 1780, asserting the practicability of a line of navigation from 'the West end of Talbutt Lane in the Parish of Whitwick' to or near Loughborough, thence to Leicester with a branch at or near Wanlip bridge to Melton Mowbray. The writer calculated that such a line would carry 50,000 tons of coal a year to Leicester and the south, and 30,000 tons to Melton and the east, plus a good trade in lime from

Barrow-on-Soar and other places on the line.[11] These figures were disputed by another correspondent who doubted the scheme's feasibility and asserted that the Loughborough Navigation proprietors would not allow their concern to become part of an unwieldy system. However, the germ of both the Leicester and the Melton Navigations lay in the scheme outlined by 'A Friend to the Public'.[12]

The project revived

For several years, the plan for a navigable waterway hung fire, while Loughborough continued to enjoy the benefits of cheap Derbyshire coal. In 1785 the price ranged between 10s. (50p) and 11s. 8d. (58½p) per ton there. Land carriage from Loughborough to Leicester added anything from 5s. (25p) to 8s. (40p) per ton to this, while other goods paid no less than 8s. 4d. (41½p) for the journey.[13]

This unsatisfactory situation obviously could not last, and the project for an extension of the waterway to Leicester was revived in the columns of the *Leicester Journal* by a correspondent who expressed surprise that it should still lie dormant in view of the fact that the Loughborough Navigation was paying 12 per cent and the Erewash Canal 15 per cent dividends.[14] The reaction was swift: a week later, it was announced that in consequence of this letter, a few individuals had set on foot a subscription to carry out this scheme, and that over £4,000 had been subscribed already.[15] An announcement soon appeared inviting would-be subscribers to notify the local banking house of Mansfield & Nutt, and implying that the promoters had not yet decided whether their navigation should go to Loughborough or directly to the Trent – probably an attempt to put a little pressure on the Loughborough Navigation, since to have two lines of waterway between the Loughborough area and the Trent would scarcely have been sensible, even if Parliament would have allowed it.[16] A private meeting of the promoters was called for 22 June 1785, but in such an ambiguous manner that a number of other interested persons turned up, and the enterprising promoters thereupon declared it an open meeting, and got promises of £13,500 in subscriptions.[17]

The scheme was by now widely known – it even got into the *Cambridge Journal* – but there was a slight delay in its progress due to William Jessop's absence in Ireland.[18] However, by mid-August he had carried out most of the survey work on the Leicester project. If there had ever been any serious intention of adopting any course other than the obvious one by way of the Soar, it had been abandoned.[19] The principal obstacles were already foreseen – there were twelve watermills on the river, the owners of all of which would have to be compensated or their mills purchased, and the new venture would undoubtedly affect the Leicestershire collieries competing for the Leicester market. Already 50,000 tons of Leicester's coal came from Derbyshire via Loughborough wharf, against 20,000 tons from the Leicestershire coalfield, and a canal to Leicester would make the position much worse.[20] The millowners and coalowners met at the Black Swan, Mountsorrel, on 14 September. Unfortunately the proceedings are not recorded, other than that it adjourned to the Three Crowns, Leicester, on 23 September.[21] Perhaps this was to finalize a concerted opposition, for by this time the navigation promoters had summoned a meeting, to which landowners and millowners were particularly invited, in Leicester on 28 September.

The importance of the project to the town was generally realized, and by permission of the sheriff, William Vann (whose house at Belgrave stood on the banks of the intended navigation), the meeting was held at Leicester Castle. The *Journal* did its best for the promoters by publishing a lengthy and reasoned editorial presenting the benefits Leicester would derive from the project. It faced the chief difficulty squarely – the opposition likely to come from the Leicestershire coalowners; the coalfield would, it said, be served by a branch canal or, if the hilly country around Coleorton prevented this, by a 'Newcastle road'. The editorial sounds as though it is based on well-informed opinion, and it may well indicate that Jessop was already contemplating the mixed canal-and-railway system which was ultimately to emerge as the disastrous Charnwood Forest line.[22]

The meeting on 28 September was attended by several of the county's most influential landowners, including Earl Ferrers and the Earls of Denbigh and Harborough, Lord Rawdon, both the county MPs (Sir John Danvers and Sir Thomas Fowke) and Charles Grave Hudson, whose opposition was ultimately to modify the line of the navigation.[23] Lord Ferrers, with considerable interests in west Leicestershire industry, was naturally opposed to the plan, but his fellow peers seem to have been unbiased. It was said at the time that the case for and against the plan was ably argued, and although Lord Rawdon (whose views probably carried more weight than any other single person) announced after examining the surveyor that he would oppose the scheme, and was followed in this by several others, it was agreed to adjourn for closer study of the project, and re-assemble at the castle on 20 October. By the time that day arrived, the promoters had managed to have Jessop's report published and distributed free to landowners, and the publicity thus gained led to a well-attended meeting, again under the chairmanship of William Vann.[24] William Heyrick, the Leicester banker, opened the case for the promoters, and received considerable support notably from the Earl of Harborough, one of the most influential figures in eastern Leicestershire. A resolution was passed that a Bill should be sought to sanction the new navigation, but then somebody brought up the question of the two branches which were already regarded as part of the scheme – one to the west Leicestershire collieries, the other to Melton Mowbray – and it was agreed to wait until the plans could be seen before taking further action.[25] Jessop was soon at work on the survey for the line to Melton, which was obviously to be a canalization of the River Wreake. Thus it was envisaged already that this part of the project, though closely connected with the main part, should be an independent venture, for subscriptions were called for it apart from the Loughborough–Leicester line, £6,000 being subscribed on the first day.[26]

The delay following the 20 October meeting allowed supporters and opponents to air their views publicly. Both fixed upon the weak point of the scheme: if it succeeded, the Leicestershire pits might well be driven out of business. One correspondent put the case very clearly in a letter to the *Journal*. It is expected, he said, that the proposed navigation would allow Derbyshire coal to be sold in Leicester at 7d. per cwt. The usual differential between Leicestershire and Derbyshire coal being 1d., the former must therefore sell at 6d. (2½p) per cwt or £1 6s. a 52 cwt. But the pit-cartload, and a narrow wheel cart would be charged 3s. (15p) road toll on its way to Leicester. Allowing 4s. (20p) for the driver's expenses, 19s. (95p) would have been spent before the coal was sold for £1 6s. (£1.30) in Leicester, leaving a profit of 7s. (35p). Out of this would have to be paid the hire of the driver, the cart, and five horses, which left insufficient to keep the trade going. But it was important that the Leicestershire pits should be kept open, as during frosts Derbyshire coal would frequently be unable to reach Leicester – he cites the preceding winter, when it could not reach Loughborough for months.[27]

Curiously enough, the promoters made little attempt publicly to counter such well-reasoned arguments, and the wilder justifications for the scheme issued by its more eccentric supporters can hardly have helped it. One advanced the mind'boggling conception of the Empress of Russia quaffing Burton beer, and another cited Scripture, somehow managing to find a parallel between Solomon's sending ships to

Tarshish and Ophir for gold and boats going to Derbyshire for coal.[28] Perhaps they did not realize the strength of the opposition which was building up, although a meeting of the plan's opponents held in Loughborough on 1 November should have warned them: it included the Earls of Huntingdon and Stamford and Earl Ferrers, Lord Rawdon, Sir John Danvers, Charles Grave Hudson and William Vann's brothers, Richard and James, as well as a number of other prominent landowners on the line. They laid plans for presenting a united front against the project at the adjourned meeting in November, and for directing operations against it in Parliament if it got that far.[29] It was all too clear that with such formidable opposition, the project's expectations of getting through Parliament were slender.

The postponed meeting was held at Leicester Castle on 24 November 1785, the chair being taken by Gerard Noel Edwards.[30] Having received approval for the main part of their scheme at the last meeting, the promoters prudently did not bring this up again, but concentrated on the possibility of serving the Leicestershire pits as well as linking with the Loughborough Navigation. They therefore got the meeting to pass a resolution asserting the advantage of a navigation between Coleorton and Loughborough, and adding that this would be even more beneficial if it were extended to Leicester and Melton Mowbray. But there was a difficulty. The Leicestershire coalowners had already produced a plan of their own, which the promoters would not accept. The petition asking for leave to bring in a Bill could not therefore be signed, and again the meeting had to be postponed, 19 January 1786 being fixed as the date by which an acceptable scheme must be received by the promoters.

It was generally accepted by now that there must be a branch to the Leicestershire collieries, controversy being merely over what tonnage might be expected to pass over it, what the effect on the Leicestershire pits would be, and whether the estimate of £26,000 for the branch was realistic.[31] The Loughborough Navigation even discussed under what terms the branch would join their own line, and what tonnages it would take.[32] That the promoters were taking active measures over the branch is shown by an announcement on 24 December that a totally new survey, along a fresh line, was being taken, and it was anticipated that this would bring more lime on to the canal. By early January 1786, the survey was completed.[33]

The long-awaited meeting to decide whether to go to Parliament was held at the castle on 29 January 1786, with William Vann in the chair. The first move was a defeat for the coalowners: Lord Rawdon proposed that a canal be made from Oakthorpe (west of Ashby-de-la-Zouch, in the western part of the Leicestershire coalfield) by way of Leicester to Melton Mowbray. Perhaps this was the coalowners' line already rejected by the promoters – if so, its second appearance had no more success than the first, for it was turned down. Instead the assembly passed resolutions favouring a canal from Thringstone Bridge by way of Loughborough to Leicester. The project for a navigation from Loughborough to Leicester only was to be given up in favour of this extended version, and the county MPs were to be asked to present a petition for a Bill, the petition being read to the assembly and approved by them.[34] On the same evening, a contented meeting of subscribers agreed to throw open the meetings of the committee directing the affairs of their project to all subscribers who cared to attend, and to buy off a troublesome piece of opposition by varying the line of the navigation to appease Charles Grave Hudson of Wanlip Hall. A call of 5 per cent was made on subscribers, and the promoters must have felt that at last matters were on the move.[35]

Failure

The degree of opposition to the scheme became more apparent as the time for the presentation of the Bill approached. Sir Charles Grave Hudson remained unpacified despite the promotors' efforts. Jessop visited him personally with the plans and invited him to sketch in a line by Wanlip he would approve; when Hudson refused to do so, a new line well away from the Hall was substituted by the promoters and the fishing rights over it granted to him. More surprising was the Loughborough Navigation's coolness to the scheme. Perhaps they were upset by the lack of any clear idea on the part of the Leicester party where their branch from the Leicestershire coalfield was to join the main line – a plan to pass south of Loughborough was apparently given up in favour of a proposal to make the junction below the second lock north of Loughborough.[36] Another possibility is that the Loughborough company were afraid of losing their position as controllers of the terminal of the waterway from the north; a contemporary accused Loughborough traders of abusing their position in this respect by holding back goods arriving from the north for Leicester until their own goods had been sold, and of keeping their prices only just below those of goods reaching Leicester by land carriage from London, whereas considerable reductions could have been made. But it may be that this accusation was made to explain away the awkward fact that only 503¼ tons of goods arrived at Loughborough wharf for Leicester in 1785, apart from the dominant article, coal.[37]

The Leicester Navigation Bill was presented in the House of Commons by John Peach Hungerford, one of the MPs for Leicestershire, on 7 April 1786.[38] Petitions in its favour were received from the mayor and corporation of Leicester, the inhabitants of Leicester (over thirteen thousand signed), and the towns of Stamford, Oakham, Uppingham, Kettering and Market Harborough. Against it, however, there were petitions from landowners, millowners, mortgagees of turnpike road tolls, Emmanuel College, Cambridge, and the Loughborough Navigation.[39] The opponents were represented at the second reading by Messrs Graham and Wood, the former of whom opened before a House of some two hundred members by roundly declaring that the main line of the navigation would ruin twelve miles of meadow land between Loughborough and Leicester, while the Thringstone branch would deprive Sir William Gordon of Garendon of the water of three brooks quite indispensable to him. A witness asserted that the brooks produced 6,000 tons of water a day – which seems more than he can possibly have required! For the Loughborough Navigation it was said that the

The typical 'double' towpath gate on the Leicester Navigation at Mountsorrel

Leicester scheme would reduce its tonnage – an unlikely event which the company's chief witness found two supporters to corroborate. More realistic were the fears expressed by one of the millers on the line, who said that there was at present not enough water for the mills on the Soar, and that a reduction of this quantity for navigation purposes would prevent them from working for much of the year.

For the promoters, the strongest witness was Jessop, who systematically refuted the opposition's assertions about damage to lands, harm to the mills, and so on. He was supported by colleagues on points of traffic potential and effect on prices. Unfortunately, the non-local members present did not find these details exciting, and as the day wore on MPs steadily drifted away in search of dinner, until by the time the division was reached, about 11 p.m., half of them had departed, leaving only those committed to one side or the other. It was a close-run thing, but the Bill was lost by fifty-one votes to forty-one. Again it seemed that all the work put into the scheme had gone for nothing. But the promoters were not disheartened: success had not been far from their grasp, and although the formalities of winding up were gone through, and the final balance of £31. 0s. 11d. (£31 ½d.) sent as a contribution to the improvement of 'Queen's Walk' (now New Walk) in Leicester, they had no intention of letting it die.[40]

This was shown by a meeting held at the Exchange in Leicester on 6 October 1786, which unanimously agreed that the scheme was of great utility. It was applauded by the *Leicester Journal*, which asserted, not wholly accurately, that the plan involved nothing more than dredging the natural channel of the river, while difficulties over towing paths and the passage of mills could easily be overcome by compensation.[41] It also hoped that a navigation would lower the price of coal in Leicester from its present 11½d. per cwt to 7d.[42] In a long editorial, the *Journal* subsequently enlarged on the latter point: land carriage from Loughborough to Leicester cost 8s. 4d. (41½p) per ton, and this should be lowered to 3s. 6d. (17½p) by water.[43] Correspondents took up the cause again, and a lengthy poem by a local bard, Charles Rozzell, introduced some rather startling comparisons to the Soar, not only with other British rivers (Thames, Severn, Trent) but also with their foreign counterparts (Seine, Loire, Garonne).[44] Not all supporters were so easily carried away: 'A Trent Navigator' from Derby was sceptical about the ease with which the Soar could be made into a satisfactory navigation, pointing out that Jessop had not yet been able to make the much larger River Trent carry 20 tons in a dry season, and the *Journal* had to admit to misrepresenting Jessop, who had said that some minor cuts would be needed.[45] However, the *Journal* found another justification for the navigation in the growing use of flagstones for paving Leicester, some of which came from as far away as Yorkshire.[46] The *Journal* pointed to the state of the Loughborough–Leicester turnpike road, which, it said, was becoming ruinous under the increasing traffic.[47] The newspaper was undoubtedly invaluable to those with the canal project at heart and must have helped to sustain interest in Leicester at a high level. It also kept up a continual running commentary on canal schemes elsewhere, including one built by 'Joseph, Prime Minister to Pharoah, King of Egypt', which, it thought, still existed.[48]

Ultimately, the agitation had its effect; and a meeting to discuss the scheme was summoned by the mayor of Leicester, Henry Watchorn, at the Town Hall on 30 October 1788, the mayor 'having received a great number of applications to call the Inhabitants together for that purpose'. Although no record exists of what transpired at the meeting, it seems probable that the supporters of the scheme received a setback, for it was stated in the Parliamentary debate on the project in the following session that it had been agreed to drop the scheme at this time. If this were the case, the reverse was not accepted by the promoters as final, for after two preliminary meetings in February 1789, a 'very full' meeting on 2 March, with Joseph Craddock of Gumley in the chair, determined to apply for an Act to sanction the scheme, and subscriptions for £14,000 were promised there and then. The plan was for a navigation from Loughborough to Leicester and Melton, and a 2 per cent call was made on the subscribers. At the same time the Loughborough Navigation was approached for its agreement to the new scheme's joining its canal 'either at Bishop's Meadow, or at a point below the first bason'. By 9 March 1789, the subscription was complete. A further call of 3 per cent was made on 2 April, and details of the proposed tonnage rates were discussed.[50]

On 13 May 1789, the scheme went before Parliament, once more introduced by John Peach Hungerford. Sir James Erskine, however, at once rose and moved that the second reading be amended to 'this day four months' instead of 'now', and although local members supported Hungerford, the amendment was carried by seventy-seven votes to thirty-seven, and the Bill was lost for that session.[51] This must have been a bitter pill for the promoters to swallow, for their Bill, which so narrowly failed in the previous session, had this time been defeated much more easily.

Success

With the hope of a reduction in the carriage of coal from Loughborough to Leicester from 5d. per cwt by land to 1½d. by water, it was unlikely that the matter would be allowed to drop; and by the end of 1789, negotiations had already begun to buy off the opposition which had overthrown the Bill.[52] The promoters were at last successful, and, following a meeting in Loughborough on 7 April 1790 at which they evidently succeeded in placating their opponents, they summoned a meeting in Leicester to consider the project afresh. This, held on 12 July 1790, announced to the world in the most convincing way possible that supporters and opponents had come to terms, for it was chaired by the most prominent of the Bill's adversaries, Lord Rawdon. The assembly resolved to apply to Parliament for powers to make a cut from the Loughborough Canal basin to the Soar; to make that river navigable thence to Leicester; and to make 'a Cut or Railway' from near Swannington or Coleorton. The scheme for a navigation to Melton Mowbray was now separated from the Leicester project, and was to go forward independently, but with the Leicester party's support. As a quid pro quo for Rawdon's cooperation, the Leicester promoters promised to support a scheme of great importance to him, the project which was ultimately to materialize as the Ashby-de-la-Zouch Canal.[53] It may well be that the Leicestershire coalowners were the more ready to withdraw their opposition to the Leicester scheme in view of the wider possibilities offered to them by the Ashby Canal. Whereas the Leicester undertaking presented them with only one sizeable market, the town itself, the Ashby was intended to join the Coventry Canal and so link the coalfield with the canal network; it seemed to present far more scope for expanding the coal trade from that area.

Jessop was at once summoned; he was in Ireland at the time, but was soon working on the proposed line between the coalfield and Loughborough.[54] He had evidently completed his preliminary draft by 4 August, when the committee supervising the operations ordered their chairman, Dr Robert Bree, a prominent advocate of waterways in Leicestershire, to report Jessop's finding to Rawdon. At the same time they appointed Christopher Staveley junior of Melton Mowbray to carry out the detailed survey for the line from Loughborough to Barrow. This partnership of Jessop and Staveley, recorded here for the first time, was to achieve their object of putting Leicester on the waterways map, and the Staveley family was to be connected with Leicestershire waterways for several decades.[55]

Rawdon having approved, the notice intimating the promoters' intention of applying to Parliament for an Act to authorize the venture appeared in the *Leicester Journal* on 10 September 1790. The main line was to run from the Loughborough Navigation near the 'bason', to join the Soar in the parish of 'Quarndon' (Quorn). Thence the river was to be made navigable as far as Cossington, where it was joined by the Wreake. Here, the line of navigation left the Soar and turned up the Wreake for over a mile, to a spot known as Turnwater Meadow, from which a cut was to be made to rejoin the Soar near Thurmaston, whence the river was to be made navigable to 'Lady's Bridge, and thence to West Bridge' in Leicester. There was also to be a branch comprising 'a rail or waggon-way, or ways, or stone road, or roads' from coal mines on Swannington Common and at Thringstone, in west Leicestershire, to Thringstone Bridge, with a branch to pits near Coleorton and Thringstone Common. From Thringstone Bridge, a canal was to be made, terminating either at Nettlebed Hill in Shepshed parish, or at the Loughborough Lane, Nanpantan, and from the termination of this a railway was to run to the basin of the navigation in Loughborough. Alternatively, the whole of this railway-and-canal system might be replaced by one consisting entirely of 'railways, waggon-ways or stone roads', in which case it was to reach the Loughborough Navigation below the first lock.

Three points are worth comment. Firstly, the departure from the Soar near Cossington was part of the penalty forced on the promoters by Hudson's determination that the navigation should not pass through his Wanlip estate. Secondly, it is interesting to note that the promoters clearly had doubts about the Forest line system of railways and canal. This may have been due either to the obvious drawbacks of the three trans-shipments of cargo between the pithead and the hold of the boat at Loughborough, or to fears over the adequacy of the water supply on the line. These qualms were to prove only too well founded, and it is interesting to speculate on what would have happened if the alternative railway line had been adopted. An efficiently worked light railway or tramroad could have handled all the traffic likely to be put on it by the Leicestershire pits and limeworks: in one year, from 1 September 1798, the Monmouthshire Canal carried 56,881 tons of goods, including 28,091 tons of coal, mostly put on it by tramroads, while the Park Mile tramroad near Newport carried 16,806 tons in the last quarter of 1810 – far more than can have been expected to come from west Leicestershire.[56]

Cossington junction, lock and weir on the Leicester Navigation

The third noteworthy feature is the termination of the canal at or near West Bridge in Leicester. Originally, the promoters seem to have intended to end their line near Lady Bridge, alongside the main road leading from Leicester to the north and east, and in fact this is where their main commercial centre, the Public Wharf at Belgrave Gate, was ultimately made. This original choice of site was no doubt dictated by considerations of cost, land in this swampy wilderness being much cheaper than in Leicester itself. But there were numerous protests; it would, it was said, be inconvenient for the townsfolk to have to come to the outskirts of Leicester for their goods, and the streets would be damaged by the increased number of heavy coal carts using them *en route* for the Public Wharf.[57] The promoters hastily gave way, and agreed to the extension to West Bridge, and even to take no additional toll on boats travelling the extra distance – a concession their successors were to regret.

The Leicester end of the line aroused controversy in other respects, too. Some critics felt that the river was not suitable for navigation purposes in and near the town, and it was even suggested that the idea should be dropped and a canal made from above the North mill, by way of Belgrave, to Birstall mill – one justification being that the cut would also act as a flood relief measure, an interesting premonition of events which were to transform the Leicester section of the navigation a century later.[58]

At the other end of the line, the question of water supplies for the Forest line worried others besides the committee. Jessop planned a reservoir in the Blackbrook valley, and the committee had to convince landowners that this would not diminish their water supply – as they wished to take some of the upper waters of the feeder streams for the reservoir, they had to guarantee an equal quantity to the Garendon estates from the reservoir itself.[59]

In view of the awkward fact that the main line of the Leicester Navigation was to be separated from the Forest line by a short stretch of the Loughborough Navigation, the promoters opened negotiations with the Loughborough, and optimistically agreed to a plan of Lord Rawdon's, by which the two concerns should unite on a profit-sharing basis; the Loughborough naturally flatly refused to consider a union on this or any other principle.[60] Jessop was consulted, and ultimately the committee offered the Loughborough a toll of 7½d. per ton on goods crossing their basin *en route* between the two separate sections of the Leicester Navigation. The Loughborough, however, were not satisfied, and asked for a guarantee of their present income of £3,000 per annum gross.

Before making another offer the Leicester promoters consulted their proprietors, drawing up two alternative schemes for their consideration. By the first, they would offer to take over the Loughborough Navigation, paying to its proprietors thereafter an annual sum equal to the average profits over the last three years. By the second, they would undertake to compensate the Loughborough for any decrease in tonnage on Derbyshire coal, lime, etc., by a toll on Leicestershire coal crossing the Loughborough.[61] The General Assembly on 24 January 1791, with Rawdon in the chair, chose the second scheme but added certain conditions – the Loughborough and Erewash were to be kept in good repair, and no tonnage was to be taken on Coleorton coal and lime crossing the Loughborough Canal. In addition the Loughborough were not to charge more than 1s. 6d. (7½p) or less than 1d. per ton on coal without the Leicester's consent, nor less than 1d per ton on any goods in a year when compensation was demanded, nor was compensation to be sought when the total quantity of coal brought along the Soar and the Forest line was less than 60,000 tons. The same meeting agreed on

[2011]

ANNO TRICESIMO PRIMO

Georgii III. Regis.

****

CAP. LXV.

An Act for making and maintaining a Navigable Communication between the *Loughborough Canal* and the Town of *Leiceſter*; and for making and maintaining a Communication by Railways, or Stone Roads, and Water Levels, from ſeveral Places and Mines to the ſaid *Loughborough Canal*; and for continuing the ſame by paſſing along the ſaid Canal, to the ſaid Navigable Communication, all in the County of *Leiceſter*.

WHEREAS the making and maintaining of a navigable Cut or Canal, to commence at or near the Baſon, above the Firſt Lock on the North Side of the Town of Loughborough in the County of Leiceſter, belonging to the Company of Proprietors of the Navigation from the River Trent to the Town of Loughborough, and to proceed from thence to the River Soar

Preamble.

22 X 2

First page of the Act of 1791 for the Leicester Navigation

tonnage rates to be sought for the Leicester Navigation, but rejected a resolution limiting their dividends to a maximum of 15 per cent.[62]

The Loughborough replied that they would not accept less than 10d. per ton compensation on coal, and reserved the right to levy their full Parliamentary rate if necessary. They rejected the proposal to dispense with compensation when less than 60,000 tons passed along the River and Forest lines, and insisted, as before, that an income of £3,000 should be guaranteed. The Leicester committee grumbled that the commissioners, to be appointed under the Act they were by now confident of getting, ought to be allowed to check whether any decreased tonnages the Loughborough reported were genuine. Also, the committee felt, if the Leicester did have to pay the Loughborough compensation, they should get their money back in the years when there was a surplus. However, they ultimately settled along the lines suggested by the Loughborough company.[63]

Another obstacle to the project's progress had been removed meanwhile: a lengthy agreement had been drawn up with Charles Grave Hudson relating to the navigation's passage through Wanlip, involving not only making an artificial cut (which was not on Hudson's land) instead of following the course of the Soar, but also taking down the watermill, for which Hudson was to be paid £500 in shares in the Leicester Navigation. There were also to be regulations governing the management of the sluice gates erected to control the waters there.[64] The Leicester Navigation was to have trouble over these regulations in later years, but the removal of the watermill was a blessing in view of the bickering between the company and the rest of the mills on the line which was so constant a feature of the navigation's history.

In due course, the Leicester Navigation Bill came before Parliament, and passed through the various stages without opposition. It received the Royal Assent on 12 May 1791.

The struggle was over, at least as far as the legal recognition of the project was concerned. After twelve years of frustration, the eagerness of the promoters to get to work on their scheme was apparent: even before the Act had passed, they were negotiating over the regulation of trade on their line, and ordering materials for its construction.[65]

CHAPTER 2

The Navigation is Made

The company's first Act: 1791

The Act (31 Geo III, c 65) opened with a comprehensive statement of the utility of the undertaking, which would, it said, link Leicester with the coalfields and limeworks, and would also open easy communications with Hull, Liverpool, Birmingham and – more surprisingly – Worcester, Gloucester and Bristol. The line authorized was the one announced by the promoters years before, the River line from near the Loughborough Navigation basin to Leicester, and the Forest line from the west Leicestershire coalfield to Loughborough. These two sections were physically entirely separate. The River line was the main line of the navigation, comprising the waterway between Loughborough and Leicester, based on the River Soar for much of its length. It was 15 miles 5 furlongs 8 chains long, and rose 50 ft by nine locks, though it subsequently proved necessary to insert an extra one (Pilling's or Barrow Flood lock) at the junction of the cut from Loughborough and the river near Barrow. This lock divided the longest pound on the navigation; the 3 miles 5 furlongs 4 chains stretch between the Junction with the Loughborough and Barrow Deep lock, the deepest lock on the line, with a fall, according to the 1790 survey, of 10 ft 1 in.[1]

All the locks were made in connection with cuts to avoid watermills, except the so-called Junction lock on the Wreake, 4 furlongs 7 chains downstream from the junction of the Leicester and Melton Navigations.

The navigation commenced some 250 yd north of the Loughborough Navigation's basin, and for the first 2½ miles was an artificial channel, which became known as the Loughborough Cut. Near Barrow, it joined the river, but before long left it by another cut which avoided Barrow mill, eliminated a lengthy meander and brought the navigation near the limeworks. Thence the course of the river was followed, with only three or four minor straightenings, to Cossington, where the Wreake flowed

Sutton's cut on the Leicester Navigation

in from the east. The line of navigation turned up the Wreake, and a considerable amount of straightening took place between here and Turnwater Meadow, where a mile and a half cut (later called 'Sutton's Cut' after a trader who established a wharf on it in the early days of the navigation) ran southward to rejoin the river at Thurmaston. From here the river, with a few minor cuts, was the route as far as Belgrave, where the main channel of the river was left, and a backwater improved as far as Belgrave Gate, where, as we have seen, the promoters originally intended to end their waterway, but were forced by public opinion to continue it.[2] The navigation therefore, followed the backwater along the Abbey Meadow to the point at which the St Margaret's Way bridge now crosses it. At this point a cut was made which joined the main course of the river, just upstream of the North mill - an expensive matter, for it forced the company to make another lock or more strictly a water level.

The Forest line consisted of a canal, with railways at both its western and eastern ends. The water level was 7 miles 6 furlongs 6 chains long and ran with no locks from Thringstone Bridge (alongside the Loughborough–Ashby-de-la-Zouch turnpike road) to Nanpantan, on the heights of Charnwood Forest above Loughborough. It had one branch, of 1 mile 5 chains from Osgathorpe entering at a distance of 2 furlongs 1 chain from Thringstone Bridge. The railways at the western end of the water level were to run from Thringstone Bridge to Swannington, Thringstone Common, and Coleorton Common, and from the Osgathorpe branch terminal to limestone quarries at Barrow and Cloud Hill. In all, there were to be 3 miles 3 furlongs 5 chains of railway at the water level's western end, though the Barrow Hill and Cloud Hill lines (7 furlongs 5 chains) were not built. At the eastern end of the water level, another railway ran down to the western side of the Loughborough Navigation's basin, this being the longest single stretch of railway on the system, at 2 miles 4 furlongs 8 chains. If the water level and railways are taken together, the Forest line was authorized as 13 miles 6 furlongs 9 chains long, against the 15 miles 5 furlongs 8 chains of the River line.

Having described the line of the navigation, the Act listed the promoters, 163 in number. They were headed by five peers – the Duke of Newcastle, the Earl of Stamford, Earl Ferrers, and Lords Rawdon and Middleton. The first and the last had extensive interests in the Notts–Derbyshire coalfield, the others were prominent Leicestershire coal-owners. The country gentry with lands on or near the line were well represented: old Leicestershire names – Beaumont, Babington, Farnham, Herrick, Pochin, Packe – appear as proprietors. Some, of course, had interests in the industry of the area to be served by the Leicester Navigation, notably Sir George Beaumont, with extensive coal and lime workings at Coleorton. One or two speculators characteristic of this period of canal mania were there – Dr Bree, for example, though he put in much solid work for the project, and William Fillingham. Leicestershire industrialists also subscribed – among them G.W. Burslem and Joseph Boultbee, and Messrs Fenton and Raper, working coalmines at Thringstone and Swannington respectively. It may be that these were reluctant participants – certainly the company had much trouble with Fenton and Raper, who flatly refused to subscribe more than the originally stipulated £100 for their shares when the company was short of money. But another industrialist who certainly subscribed willingly, with a view to extending his business rather than making a fortune out of his canal investment, was Edward Miller Mundy of the Shipley colliery in Derbyshire. Some traders on the Loughborough Navigation became proprietors of the present canal, too, notably Messrs Douglass and Ella. But the main strength of the new company lay in its Leicester subscribers, who included the leading figures in the financial and professional life of the town (Messrs Bentley and Buxton, Boultbee, Mansfield, Pares, Heyrick), as well as the leaders of the business community and civic affairs – no fewer than six of the Bankart family, for instance.

In addition to the railways authorized by the Act, the proprietors of the Leicester Navigation were also given powers to make such other tramroads as they thought fit to coal, lime, and other works near the canal, these lines not to exceed 2,000 yd in length. Conversely, landowners with mineral workings on their estates could build tramroads to the navigation.

In view of doubts regarding water supplies on the Forest line, the company's powers to take water from streams were rigorously limited. They were allowed to do so from the Swannington and Thringstone Brooks, and they could take water from other springs which were within 2,000 yd of the canal, but should the planned reservoir be required it was only to be built on the site specified in the Act. They were not to draw water from the Gracedieu Brook or its feeders, and they were to ascertain the average flow of the Blackbrook and keep this up by supplying it from the water level. They could place a waste weir where their canal crossed the Blackbrook and nowhere else. However, they were allowed to take, as of right, water raised from any mine within 2,000 yd of the line by any 'Fire Engine, Machine, or Level', and owners of mines boating their coal along the canal were required to pump the water from their mines into the canal.

There were fewer problems over water on the River line, though the water supply to Rawdon's two mills in Loughborough was safeguarded. The major limitation on the course of the line was that the cut from Turnwater Meadow to Thurmaston was not to be nearer than 575 yd to Wanlip Hall. At the Loughborough end, the company were empowered to make a junction with the Loughborough Navigation, and required to make 'a proper and sufficient Drawbridge or Swivel Bridge' over the junction. Boats were to be allowed to pass over the 300 yd of Loughborough Navigation dividing the Forest line tramroad and the River line, subject to the terms already negotiated between the two companies.[4]

The capital authorized to pay for the entire project was limited to £46,000 in shares of not more than £100 in value. A further £20,000 could be raised by the issue of new shares or by mortgaging the tolls. Subscribers were to be paid 5 per cent interest on their shares until the navigation was opened, beginning as soon as the first £25 call on each share had been paid. The tonnage rates the company could charge were limited to the following maxima:

	Per ton			Per ton-mile
	s.	d.	(p)	d.
Coal from the Loughborough Navigation: to Leicester	1	2	(6)	
to any intermediate part of the Leicester Navigation (excluding coal passing on to the Melton Navigation)				1
to the intended Melton Navigation		7		
Iron, timber and other goods from the Loughborough Navigation: to Leicester	2	6	($12\frac{1}{2}$)	
to intermediate points	1	3	(6)	
Lime, limestone, stone or other building or road making materials	half the coal rate			
Coal along the Forest line to Loughborough				$1\frac{1}{2}$
Lime and limestone along the Forest line railways				$1\frac{1}{2}$
Lime and limestone along the Forest line water level				$\frac{3}{4}$
All other goods along the Forest line railways and water level				2

Fractions of a ton were to be paid for by the quarter ton. All manure, except lime, used to improve lands through which the navigation ran, and all materials for mending local roads, were to pass toll-free except through locks when water was not running to waste. Tolls on goods passing on to the Melton Navigation were not to exceed half those on goods from Loughborough to Leicester.

An interesting clause shows that the company were envisaging container traffic on the Forest line. It laid down that where the owners of limeworks intended to send their product along the line in 'Carriages, Boxes, or Cases appropriated to that Purpose', they should be of a kind approved by the company, whose officers were to gauge the quantity the containers would hold, and mark them accordingly. After this the toll charged would always be for that quantity, regardless of how much lime the cases really contained. If the lime went directly into a boat with no container, a bill of lading was required to accompany it, and the charge would be based on this.

Three other clauses were to prove an embarrassment to the company, one temporary, the others for a longer period. The first forbade opening any part of the navigation for the conveyance of coal until the whole complex was finished; a small part of the Forest line only was exempted as it would serve as a local communication between Leicestershire coalmines and limeworks. The idea was, of course, to prevent the River line from opening before the Forest line and so enable the Derbyshire coalowners to establish command of the Leicester market before their Leicestershire rivals could compete. The second clause ordered the company to guarantee the tolls of the Ashby to Leicester turnpike road (an impoverished concern, £3,975 in debt) at the figure of £300 a year, and the third forced them to give a similar guarantee to the Markfield–Whitwick road, of £40 a year.

There was also the usual sprinkling of clauses regulating the settlement of the disputes which would inevitably arise between the company on the one hand, and the landowners, millowners, and boatmen on the other, and the usual enormous number of commissioners was named to resolve them. But there was little in the Act the proprietors had cause to regret in the long run – except the important matter of tonnage rates, which within a few years showed themselves to have been fixed optimistically low.

Construction

The lengthy period between the inception of the scheme, its development, and the Act at least ensured that the company had a construction team well aware of the difficulties at hand. Their engineer, William Jessop, was by then a recognized leader in his profession. His surveyor, Christopher Staveley junior, must by now have known the proposed line intimately. There was also a semi-official helper, William Keightley

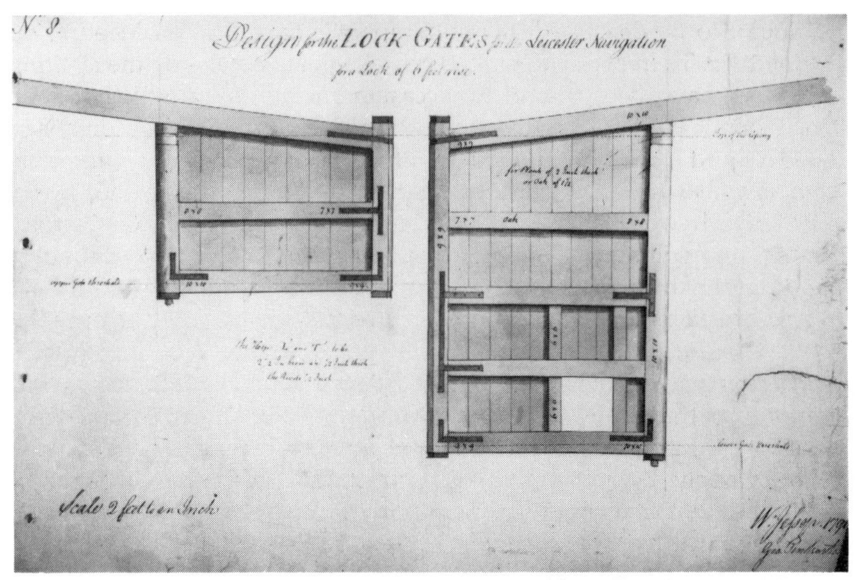

Design for lock gates on the Leicester Navigation, signed by William Jessop and George Pinkerton in 1791

or Keatley (the name appears in a variety of forms), who, although a blacksmith by trade, was able to take levels and handle the surveyor's chain, in addition to finding construction materials and tradesmen; he saved much of Jessop's time and hence the company's money. Jessop subsequently recommended him to the Nottingham promoters' canal.[5] Both Jessop's helpers did well for themselves; Staveley was described at the time of his death in 1827 as a 'deservedly respected' architect and surveyor, and Keightley, who also died in 1827, remained an engineer for the rest of his life.[6]

Work had already begun on collecting constructional materials before the Act was passed, a call of 3 per cent being made to cover this.[7] Keightley soon found three brickmakers along the line who between them contracted for a total of 450,000 bricks at an average price of £1 1s. (£1.05) per thousand. The committee meanwhile pondered on the best way to start work, thinking it might be best to carry out the works between Barrow and Leicester, thereby opening a trade in lime from the former, while also starting work on the Forest line with such labour as they could get. They decided to ask Jessop's advice on this, and would-be contractors were invited to 'deliver their proposals' to the engineer, to be discussed at the company's first General Meeting on 1 June 1791. There were no immediate takers, however, and the meeting seems to have been more an occasion for self-congratulation than discussion.[8] The advertisement was therefore repeated in a number of London and provincial papers, with a closing date of 4 July. The company also invited tenders for the road bridges along the line, nearly all of which would have to be rebuilt. All those interested in their upkeep and willing to share the cost were then invited to a committee meeting at which the tenders were to be inspected. Along the line, would-be sellers of land were already stressing its added value once the navigation was open.[9]

It seems that by now it was widely believed that the company planned to minimize trans-shipment of cargoes on the Forest line, for the *Leicester Journal* of 1 July 1791 printed a long article, unfortunately anonymous but obviously by somebody with practical engineering experience, proposing that coal should be transported from the pits to the canal in wagons which could be rolled direct on to rail tracks on the canal boats. The wagons were to be 6 ft long by 3 ft wide by 4 ft high, running on four 2 ft-diameter flanged wheels. The procedure for getting the wagons on to the boats was described in some detail. The boat, with two sets of rails fastened to its floor timbers, was to be moored stern-on to the wharf, held in position by rows of piles projecting from the canal bed. The wagon was to be manhandled on to the boat by means of a turntable on the wharf and a movable flap on to the boat's stern. It was then to be winched along the rails to the fore-end of the boat, and the process repeated until the boat carried its full complement of twenty wagons.

On arriving at the other end of the canal, the boat would moor with its fore-end to the wharf, and the wagons would be winched out along movable flaps and so transferred to rail for the next stage of their journey.

Quite why the writer thought it worthwhile sending, or the *Journal* printing, such a semi-technical article is not clear, though it certainly seems to have staggered the *Journal*, which found it 'hitherto UN-PRECEDENTED' to transport wagons by boat, dismissing ferryboats as irrelevant. One would have thought the chairman of the Leicester Navigation company a more suitable recipient. Perhaps it was meant to arouse controversy at the imminent General Meeting, on 4 July 1791. If so, it does not appear to have succeeded, for the meeting concerned itself with necessary matters like electing clerks (John Edward Carter and John Heyrick Junior) and treasurers (Messrs Boultbee and Mansfield

Three Cranes Inn, Leicester,
July 4th 1791.

At a General Assembly of the Proprietors for putting into Execution an Act passed in the thirty first Year of his present Majesty intitled "An Act for making and maintaining "a navigable Communication between the Loughborough Canal and the "Town of Leicester; and for making and maintaining a .... "Communication by Railways or Stone Roads and Water levels from "several places and Mines to the said Loughborough Canal, and for "continuing the same by passing along the said Canal to the said "navigable Communication all in the County of Leicester," — Present

William Pochin Esq in the Chair

Dr Bree, M.B. — John Mansfield Esq
Joseph Boultbee Esq — Mr Thomas Swinburn
Thomas Farnham Esq — Revd Thomas Willows
Thomas Charlton Esq — Mr Thomas Prest
Mr Alderman Burbidge — Mr John Cradock

Opening of the minutes of the General Assembly on 4 July 1791 of the proprietors of the Leicester Navigation

and Bentley and Buxton). A committee of thirteen was elected, Leicester interests predominating, but also including representatives of the land-owners and the traders. Curiously, the Assembly found time to design itself a coat of arms: azure, a chevron gules between three urns. In fact they got their heraldry wrong; the red chevron on a blue field commits the solecism of placing one colour on another. They also adopted a motto, taken, with a delightfully Georgian touch, from Horace: *Liquidus fortunae rivus inauret* (May the liquid stream of fortune cover you with gold), a tag from the *Epistles*, XII, line 9. They also adopted a crest to accompany the coat of arms – a cornucopia proper, to symbolize the good things the navigation was to shower on the public.

Although there can have been little doubt about who was to supervise the navigation's construction, it was left to the committee on 5 July 1791 to formally appoint Jessop engineer at £350 per annum, including expenses, and Staveley as surveyor at £200 per annum, also including expenses. As the same meeting had to authorize payments for £2,263,

LXXIX. And it is hereby further enacted, That it ſhall be lawful for the Owner or Owners, Occupier or Occupiers of any Lands adjoining to the ſaid Navigation or Water Levels, to uſe any Pleaſure Boat or Boats thereon, not paſſing through any Lock, unleſs they ſhall pay Tonnage equal to a Boat or Veſſel carrying Twenty Tons, or obtain the Conſent of the ſaid Company of Proprietors, without Interruption from the ſaid Company of Proprietors, and without paying any Rate or Duty for the ſame, ſo as ſuch Pleaſure Boat or Boats be not made uſe of for carrying Goods, Wares, or Merchandizes, and ſo as the ſame do not obſtruct or prejudice the Navigation of the ſaid Rivers, Canals, and Water Levels, or Towing Paths on the Sides thereof.

Land Owners may uſe Pleaſure Boats.

Paragraph from the Leicester Navigation Act of 1791 allowing owners of adjacent land to use pleasure boats on the water levels

they also made a call on shares of 5 per cent.[10] The committee had also begun to have justifiable doubts about the size of their capital, and on 21 July 1791, they ordered it to be raised from £46,000 to £50,700, and added a list of the 164 subscribers and the amounts for which they had accepted responsibility. The largest shareholder was Lord Rawdon with £2,000, followed by Dr Bree with £1,200, and Mary Wynne of Gumley with £1,100. Among the proprietors with £1,000 were the Lords Stamford and Ferrers, Joseph Boultbee, and Messrs Bentley and Buxton. The country landowners in the list were mostly resident on or near the line, but Charles Simpson of Launde Abbey, in a remote part of the eastern border of Leicestershire, subscribed £400. By far the greater part of the money was to come from local sources – Leicestershire itself, or the adjacent counties.

On 27 July, the committee finally decided to push on with the canal section of the Forest line – not because this section would be more difficult to make than the River line, and so should be started first if the two were to be opened at the same time – but because the lands around the River line were under corn for which the company would have to pay if work began before the harvest. Work on the River line was for the time being confined to having the lands valued. The committee even sold off some of the bricks they had already gathered at Thurmaston. Staveley's plan for the navigation from Loughborough to Leicester and to Melton Mowbray was already on sale in Leicester, and the company sent a bill for one third of the cost of this survey to the Melton Navigation company as their share. The enthusiastic Keightley came forward with his own ideas for a line, and was snubbed by Jessop – an unusual action for that amiable character. On 15 September 1791, the committee ordered another call of 10 per cent so that one fifth of their capital was now called up.

Details of the contract under which the main line of the navigation was constructed are not preserved. The draft was discussed by the committee on 1 September 1791 and sealed on 29 September, the firm with whom they were negotiating being Messrs Pinkerton; presumably George, James and Francis Pinkerton, with whom a separate agreement over the railways was reached in the following year (see below).[11] From the first payments made to the firm for work done, it appears that, apart from the usual 5 per cent retention held back as a guarantee of good work, £1,000 of the contract sum was to lie in the company's hands until two years after completion of the undertaking.[12]

The date when the Pinkertons began work was not recorded, but on 20 October 1791 the committee sold them the bricks it had at Thring-

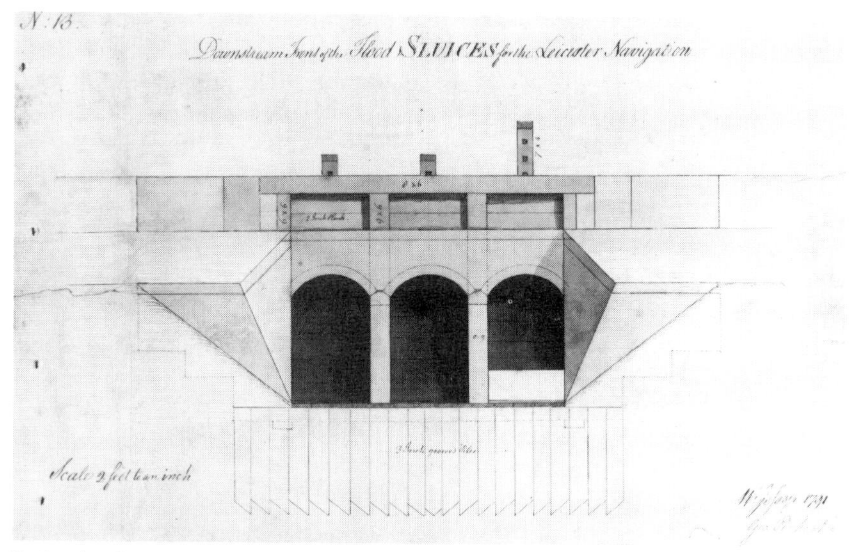

Design for downstream front of sluices by William Jessop and George Pinkerton, 1791

stone Bridge and Gracedieu, and Staveley reported on 1 November that they had carried out work to the value of £303 on the site.[13] The Pinkertons proceeded to push ahead with the work, although bad weather slowed down operations towards the end of the year, and a further 5 per cent call was made to meet the mounting expenditure. So well did matters go that early in 1792 the Pinkertons were running short of materials, and the company sold them 57,000 bricks they had procured in the Wanlip-Syston area. A further call of 5 per cent was made on 20 July 1792.

Early in 1792, it was decided to put work in hand on the Forest line railways, and a draft agreement with the Pinkertons was reached on 3 February. The final contract, however, was not drawn up until 6 July 1792 – surprisingly, for by that time, the company had reason to doubt the Pinkertons' ability to finish the River line on time. They had already had to make a loan of £200 to the Pinkertons to enable them to keep up their progress, and a further £250 in May, while the General Meeting on 2 July agreed to the committee's proposal that the Pinkertons should be offered a bonus of £50 for every week the navigation was open before the contract date of 23 September 1793.[14]

The Forest line railways

The contract for the construction of these, the most celebrated, if ephemeral, feature of the Leicester Navigation, was let on 6 July 1792, the contractors being George, James and Francis Pinkerton, for £7,847. For this, they undertook to make all the railways involved, scheduled as follows (sums rounded to the nearest pound sterling):

	yd	£
Loughborough to the commencement of the water level	4,587	3,208
Cloud Hill	1,628	1,187
Thringstone Bridge–Swannington Common	1,738	1,240
Branch from this to Coleorton	1,373	1,002
Two terminal branches to Coleorton branch	1,373	650
Barrow Hill	132	91
30 passing places, 25 yd each	750	469

These were to be finished on or before 29 September 1793, and the

Pinkertons were to maintain them for a further six months. Payment was to be made by instalments, as the work progressed, on the engineer's certificate, the company retaining 5 per cent of the amount due as a guarantee against bad work, and paying these retentions six months after completion. Alterations required by the company during construction could be charged for by the Pinkertons if they increased the cost, and allowed for in their demand for payment if they reduced it. Work not done to the satisfaction of the company's engineer was to be put right at the Pinkertons' own expense. In case of extreme dissatisfaction, the company could take the works out of the Pinkertons' hands and finish them themselves, the Pinkertons allowing them the expense thus incurred.

The contract goes into interesting detail about the construction of the railways, though unfortunately any plans and drawings which once accompanied it are now missing. Cuttings were to be 12 ft wide at base, and the sides sloped so that one foot horizontal traverse was matched by one foot vertical rise. Embankments were to be 15 ft wide at the top, with sides sloped to give a 1 ft fall for each 1 ft 6 in horizontal traverse. A trench 2 ft deep was to be dug under each rail, and filled with closely-packed stone. Embankments were to be well rammed before this was done, and at passing places the depth and width of the trenches were to be reduced to 18 in. Sleepers were to be of oak, 6 ft long, 7 in wide, and 3 in thick, with a 'pad' or 'piece' 12 in long and of the same section laid at each end and fastened to the sleeper by oak pins. Each sleeper was to be firmly underpinned by stones upon the foundation. The rails were to be cast iron, 3 ft long, and 28 lb in weight. Ballast was to be laid between sleeper and rail, with a convex surface. The lines were to be single track, with 25 yd-long passing places at 400 yd centres.[15]

This may be the place to say that, despite the apparent wealth of detail recorded in the contract, there is still considerable doubt about some features. The gauge is unrecorded; however, if one assumes that the rails were laid on the centre of the wooden 'pads' occupying the outside foot of each end of the sleepers, this would give a gauge of between 4 ft 8 in and 4 ft 10 in. With regard to the rails themselves, the old view that they were the first edge rails laid anywhere has been disproved, but it is generally thought that they were the first fish-bellied edge rails. If the specimens in Leicestershire Museums claiming to be from the Forest line really are so, then this was the case. Unfortunately, documentation is inadequate, and their associations give rise to doubts. Suspicion is also aroused by a description of the rails given by W.A. Provis in his survey of 1832, about which more will be said later. The crucial words are: '. . . the cast Iron *Plates* having many joinings, their surfaces being rougher, *and a larger portion being in contact with the wheel'* (author's italics); in other words, the rails had a broad bearing surface. Provis went on to imply that they had a broader bearing surface than the rails of the Liverpool and Manchester Railway, on which steam locomotives were hauling loads far heavier than anything ever put on the Leicester Navigation's railways. The surviving rails attributed to the Forest line railways have a very tenuous bearing surface indeed, far slighter than the Liverpool and Manchester rails. In fact, Provis' report reads remarkably as though he were describing, not edge rails, but tramplates. One is forced to one of three conclusions; that either Provis never saw the rails of the Forest line, but assumed that they were tramplates, or that the rails said to be from the Forest line are not so, or that the line had been relaid by 1832.

The company takes over

In the summer of 1792, public confidence in the scheme continued unabated, despite clear evidence of trouble on the work: five shares on which £40 had been paid were auctioned for £774, the highest price paid for a single share being £163. By August, the shares stood at £153–5, and some fetched even higher prices. No doubt the sight of activities beginning in Leicester itself stimulated this: the company gave notice to the owners of property in the Northgate area to have their buildings required for the navigation vacated, and the owner of the Leyroes (where the company intended to establish their Public Wharf and which they intended to buy) was told to set about making wharves, or the company would do it for him at his expense. The consequence was an outburst of activity on the banks of the Soar as wharves and factories were constructed in anticipation of the navigation's arrival.[16] Another effect was the promotion of a new venture to extend the line south of Leicester, eventually to materialize as the Leicestershire and Northamptonshire Union Canal.[17]

But the committee was not happy about the Pinkertons' progress. They had already contemplated taking the work out of the contractors' hands, and when an arrangement for the purchase of wood for the latter's use was made, they were careful to insert clauses safeguarding the material if the contractors should 'desert or be dismissed'. On 2 August 1792, they issued an ultimatum, instructing Jessop to give the Pinkertons ten days notice of a general inspection. If he then required alterations and these were not carried out, he was to report to the committee that the firm was incompetent, and the work would be taken into the company's hands. On 25 August, they emphasized their dissatisfaction by refusing to advance any more money to the contractors until Staveley reported that they had earned it.

It did not take Jessop long to decide that the contractors were unsatisfactory: he reported this to a special committee meeting on 29 August 1792, and the committee at once ordered that Staveley should take direct charge of the works.[18] The committee tried to get John Braithwaite, perhaps the father of the John Braithwaite of the Rainhill locomotive trials and engineer of the Eastern Counties Railway, to take charge of the railway's construction, but without success, and it was probably overseen by William Reed, appointed to superintend the workmen on the project with effect from 7 September 1792. A call of 10 per cent had already been made on 9 November in view of the need for pressing on the languishing works. This meant that 40 per cent of the capital was called up. The Pinkertons were finally paid off on 17 January 1793. The company thus had its hands free, but clearly the rise in prices during the French Revolutionary War was embarrassing them, for they found it necessary to make a further call of 10 per cent on 1 March and another on 11 May 1793.

In Leicester itself, there was some suspicion that the company intended to avoid or at least shelve, making the section from the Public Wharf to West Bridge, and to devote their activities to developing wharves around the former instead; some of their shareholders, indeed, were tactless enough to admit that this was the case.[19] To allay these doubts, a valuation of the property needed by the company in the West Bridge area was made, the owners of the lands required being promised 5 per cent interest on the purchase price until the latter was paid, and Reed was ordered to put his labour force on to demolishing buildings on the line. Immediately after this, the committee made another 10 per cent call, so that by now 70 per cent of the capital was called up. Work was proceeding satisfactorily along the line, to such an extent that the Leicestershire coalowners were asked if they were willing to allow the navigation to be opened for coal when the Forest line was completed and the River line to Leicester only partly opened.[20] No record of their answer is preserved, but clearly it was unfavourable, perhaps because the committee vaguely specified 'a proper Communication for the carriage of Coal' instead of stating that the Forest line system as planned would be opened. A week later, the committee ordered Staveley to press on as fast as possible with work on the Loughborough to Leicester section, except for the work in Leicester itself, and to cut down activity on the Forest line to work necessary to preserve what had been done already from the rigours of the next winter.

Jessop gave his opinion that it would be best to push on with building the locks until all were four feet high; they could then be completed individually at the company's convenience. Staveley, who could probably have done without the extra work as he was just getting married, found himself bombarded with directives. He was to obtain more bricks and prepare new schedules of work for the bricklayers, to get more timber, to see that nobody made off with any of the surplus building materials the company were selling from the Abbey Meadow, Leicester, and finally to answer a lengthy questionnaire which included the blunt and embarrassing question 'Why are the bricks so bad?' They were also expensive; a bricklayer had told the committee that 9 tons of coal should fire 20,000 bricks, whereas their returns showed that 300 tons of coal had been used for only 260,000 bricks, and they wanted to know why. The committee also suspected both the quality and the quantity of timber their supplier, Oldham, was sending, and Staveley was ordered to investigate this too. The hard-pressed Staveley delayed answering for a month, despite a barrage of demands from the committee, but eventually managed to explain the discrepancy.

The General Meeting on 6 July 1793 heard a report from the committee to the effect that the railways were 'in a considerable forwardness', the line between Leicester and Loughborough nearly finished, and work, at least on the main line, going ahead well. About 350 workmen were employed.[21] The committee had, however, sounded a warning note about finance, saying that special arrangements would have to be made to raise money if the works were to continue at the same speed. They managed to avoid this for the moment, but three further calls of 10 per cent each on 12 July, 12 September and 8 November meant that the whole of their capital had been called up before the end of 1793, with no part of their navigation opened – though Jessop believed, wrongly as it turned out, that the Loughborough to Leicester section might be open before Christmas.[22] Whether Jessop meant the whole stretch to West Bridge is unknown, but Staveley had already been ordered to begin work on the North lock, and the contract for the road bridge at that lock (an important work, as the main road from the north entered the town over it) was let to Thomas Gooddess, whose bricklayers received 3s. (15p) a day. At the same time, the committee launched a campaign to

Iron Work for One Lock

For the Sells	Long		Weight lbs
4 Bolts with flat head & nut & Screw	5..0 × 3/4 Square		36.
16 Jagged dowells	1..2 × 3/4 square		34
2 Myter plates	3..6	3 × ½	34
14 Spikes	0..6	½ Inch sq	6
			110 — 110
Upper Gates			
6 Hoops	2..6	2½ × ½	61
8. L's	2.6	2½ × ½ =	81
4 T's	3.0	2½ × ½ =	49
4 Straps	6..0	2½ × ½ =	98
2 Collars	4.0	2½ × ½	32 ½
10. Rivits	0..10.	½ Inch square	7 ¼
30 do	0..9.	½ Inch sq.	19
			348. 348
Lower Gates			
6 Hoops	as above		61.
8. L's			81.
4. T's			49.
4 double T's			
4. Straps	7..6	2½ × ½	122.
2 Collars			98.
			32 ½
24 Rivits	0.10	½ Square	10 ½
42 do	0.9	½ do	26
			480. 480
	Cwt.. qrs. lbs		
	8.. 1.. 22		946

Specification for the ironwork of a lock on the Leicester Navigation

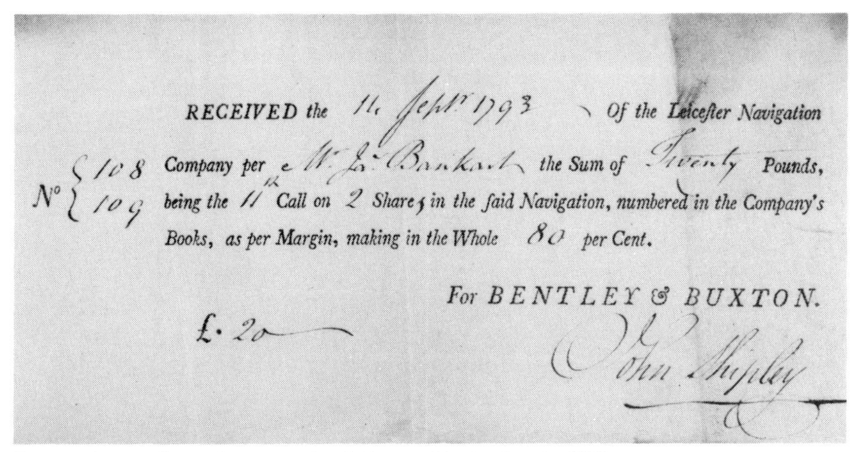

RECEIVED the 11 Septr 1793 Of the Leiceſter Navigation

No {108 / 109} Company per Mr. [illegible] the Sum of Twenty Pounds, being the 11 Call on 2 Shares in the ſaid Navigation, numbered in the Company's Books, as per Margin, making in the Whole 80 per Cent.

For BENTLEY & BUXTON.

£. 20

John Shipley

Receipt for a call on shares on the Leicester Navigation in 1793

recover the company's barrows, planks, tools, etc., looted from the works – on a large scale and along the whole line, to judge from the fact that five agents were appointed to supervise the recovery, at Loughborough, Sileby, Thurmaston, Belgrave and Leicester.

Expenditure was heavy on account of the rapidity with which work was being carried on, and the committee was eventually forced to borrow from its treasurers. Among the major items purchased were two cargoes of iron from Joseph Butler of Chesterfield which were presumably rails for the Forest line, some of which proved unsatisfactory in service.[23] By 8 November, some at least of the railways were in use, and Staveley was ordered to lay down an additional, temporary railway at the Blackbrook valley to assist in making the embankment there.[24] The pace slackened towards the end of the year, as parts of the navigation were completed and materials were sold off. On 6 December, Staveley reported that only seven bridges remained to be built, all on the Forest line. Whether the rapidity of the construction work took the Leicestershire coalowners by surprise, or whether they were dragging their feet in the hope of better transport facilities in the west of the county is not known but it became clear that the Forest line was likely to be ready for use before they were ready to use it. Jessop, accordingly, was ordered to write to the leading coal lessees, Fenton and Raper and Boultbee, asking whether, in view of their unreadiness, they would object to coal being allowed to pass over the Leicester–Loughborough line before the Forest line opened. The reply of the first company is not recorded, but was obviously not a flat refusal, while Boultbee was non-committal – as a tenant at will of Sir George Beaumont, he was in a delicate position. The committee returned to the attack, which was important to them, since the first section of the navigation, from Loughborough to Sileby, was opened probably in early December, while the first boat reached Mountsorrel in mid-December.[25] Rather belatedly, the company appointed a toll collector, John Ella, for this part of their project, with effect from 1 January 1794. He was to give £200 security, and pay his receipts fortnightly to the treasurers. By the time he took up his duties, the navigation was on the point of being opened as far as the junction with the Melton Navigation.

The committee evidently anticipated that the navigation would be opened to Leicester in mid-February, for they hurriedly placed an order for a weighing machine for the wharf there, stipulating that it must be ready within six weeks. They also faced the fact that they had spent £51,229 on the work so far, including Parliamentary expenses, and required a further £15,000 to complete it.[26] Although they had already been authorized by the previous General Meeting to raise money by mortgaging the tolls, they were reluctant to do this, and produced two alternative schemes for the approval of the General Meeting held on 6 January 1794. However, that meeting rejected both, and ordered that the extra money should be raised by a voluntary subscription among the proprietors in proportion to their holdings. If any proprietors refused to take part, their portion of the increase was to be disposed of at a special meeting. They also ordered that as soon as the main line was open, coal should be allowed along it, and the unsold stock of the Leicestershire coalowners mined after the opening should be bought by the company. These may have been the terms laid down by Fenton and Raper in a letter of 4 January, for the clerks were ordered to reply to this and to point out that the coalowners were showing no signs of any preparations to use the railways.[27]

The 6 January meeting was also told why work on the main line and the Forest line (expected to open in two and four months respectively) had fallen behind schedule and exceeded Jessop's estimate: labour was dearer, the Pinkertons had failed to carry out their contract, and the committee had been forced to order the widening and deepening of several places in the Leicester section of their line to accommodate the vessels of Grand Junction size which were expected to use the line once the Leicestershire and Northamptonshire Union Canal was completed.[28]

To give the proprietors time to think about the voluntary contribution, the meeting was then adjourned to 27 January. On that date, the twenty-two shareholders present agreed to raise the £15,000 by calling on all subscribers to pay an extra £30 on each £100 share.[29] The first call, of £10 per share, was made on 1 February 1794.

The opening of the Leicester Navigation

Meanwhile preparations for dealing with trade in Leicester were going ahead against the day of the navigation's opening: Ella, Douglass and Poynton announced the setting up of their new wharf near West Bridge, and their intention of carrying to Gainsborough, Yorkshire, Lincolnshire, Nottingham, Newark, Shardlow, Derby, Birmingham and the Erewash and Cromford Canals, and to Market Harborough as soon as the Union Canal was opened. Richard Braithwaite of Leicester informed the public that he would build boats for the navigation of 30 to 50 tons burthen, drawing no more than 3½ ft when laden; and by 14 March two coal boats were actually brought up to Leicester for sale near the North Bridge.[30] Staveley produced plans for completing the coal wharf. In the event, however, the carriage of coal was delayed. The Leicestershire coalowners were quite willing to allow the main line to be opened for the transport of coal before the Forest line, provided the company bought their unsold coal. But there was a snag: if the company bought the coal, they would have to transport it to Loughborough by road. This would cost 2d. per cwt, amounting to £300 a week on the Leicestershire pits' weekly output of 1,800 tons. As this was more than the company was likely to receive from tolls on the main line, the plan was quietly dropped.[31]

If the company could not have Leicestershire coal coming on to their own line immediately, they were determined that nobody else should get it. It has already been pointed out that one reason for the Leicestershire coalowners' reluctance to spend money on equipment for using the Forest line railways was that they still had hopes for alternative transport arrangements, and in particular for the Ashby-de-la-Zouch Canal. In its original form, this scheme posed a very real threat to the Forest line, being reasonably accessible from the mining areas of Coleorton and Swannington, and the company therefore acted swiftly. They insisted that the Ashby company should insert a clause in their Bill imposing a stiff toll on coal passing from the Coleorton–Swannington area onto the Ashby – though owing to later amendments to the Ashby's line, this clause never became operative. Other clauses were forced on the Ashby to prevent them from taking water which would otherwise feed the Forest line water level. In making these demands the company were fortified by the support of the former Lord Rawdon, who became Earl of Moira on the death of his father in 1793. He no doubt saw the injustice of forcing the company to build the Forest line and then destroying its traffic potential.

When the main line opened, therefore, it was for goods other than coal, and evidently the committee did not regard this as worthy of formal celebration – in fact, so unobtrusively did the Loughborough to Leicester line come into the world that local papers disagreed both about the actual date and the first arrival. The *Journal* asserted that the navigation opened on 22 February 1794, and that the first arrivals were two boats with goods from Gainsborough; the *Leicester Herald* claimed it opened the day before, when a single Gainsborough boat arrived. Both papers, however, united in demanding an 'accommodation' between the coalowners and the company so that coal could move along the navigation immediately.[32] Despite this, even the non-coal traffic stopped later in the month, when a flood damaged the bridge at Cossington.[33] This was soon repaired, but traffic probably did not restart until late March: W. Keightley announced in the *Journal* that he had 'this day' (i.e. 28 March) received the first boatload of lime along the navigation from Barrow-on-Soar.[34]

It seems that rumours were soon being spread by boatmen that the locks were in some way defective – the only specific charge which can be disentangled is that they were of different widths – and this came to the ears of the committee, who promptly wrote to Jessop asking him, in effect, why the locks were so badly designed and what was the maximum width of boat which could pass all the locks without damage to either itself or the locks. Later he was asked to make a survey of the locks and report whether they were executed according to his plans. It would seem that Jessop was able to smooth matters over, for no report survives.

With the end of their task in sight, the committee were scraping the bottom of the barrel to raise money for the completion of the work. Calls of £10 and £5 a share were made on those who voluntarily agreed to pay the extra 30 per cent on their holdings in April and June respectively, materials which were not immediately required – like thirty thousand bricks in one of the brickyards – were sold, and stern letters were written to those in arrears. Tolls, naturally, were still minute: Ella's takings up to the end of March 1794 amounted to no more than £20 13s. 6d. (£20.67½). Despite the extra calls there was still not enough to finish the construction so on 7 July 1794 the General Meeting, told that £65,570 had been spent already and another £6,000 was needed, agreed to raise it by borrowing as much from the treasurers as they would lend, and getting the rest elsewhere, perhaps by persuading creditors to extend the period of their loans.

Operational methods were discussed and, on Jessop's recommendation, it was decided to appoint toll collectors at the junction of the two western arms of the Forest line water level, near Osgathorpe, the junction of the Leicester and Loughborough Navigations, the flood lock near Barrow-on-Soar, the junction with the Melton Navigation, and Leicester. Toll-houses were to be built at the Osgathorpe collecting point and Loughborough, but the toll collecting at the junction with the Melton could be done by an employee of the latter, the committee hoped. Tolls were now mounting rapidly as trade increased; Barrow-on-Soar lime and Welsh slates were soon on offer in Leicester, and wool and cheese were travelling north.[35] By 7 July 1794, £220 had been

Junction of the Loughborough and the Leicester Navigations

collected. A boom was ordered to be placed across the entrance of the Leicester Navigation in Loughborough so that Ella could more effectively gauge boats coming on to the waterway. Three toll collectors were appointed on 1 August 1794: George Webb at Leicester, William Swinburne at Loughborough, and John Gildart on the Forest line. All were to be paid £40 per annum and to give £200 security. Ella was instructed to hand over his account books to Swinburne. Michael Middleton, who had also been acting as a temporary toll collector, paid over his receipts of £17 17s. 4d. (£17.87) on 8 August.

It was high time that the navigation was opened for coal traffic: there was evidently public dissatisfaction, although when this appeared in the press, the committee were able to show that their hands were tied by their Act. To make matters worse, it was widely known that the coalowners had done practically nothing to prepare to use the line. Fenton and Raper and Boultbee obviously had very little time for it, and had flatly refused to pay the voluntary £30 on their shares. Another thorn in the company's flesh reappeared. Sir Charles Grave Hudson, suspiciously watching constructional activities from his mansion at Wanlip, saw what he thought was a diversion of the river being made at the junction with the cut from the Wreake but the committee were able to reassure him that it was only work being done to enable boat horses to ford this point more easily.

It must, therefore, have been with deep satisfaction that the committee on 24 October 1794 passed a resolution that 'the Navigation is now open for the Carriage of Coals according to the Tenor of the Act of Parliament'. This followed a report by their chairman, Thomas Deakin, a committee member called Nichols, and Christopher Staveley, that a boatload of coal from Burslem's collieries at Coleorton had passed along the Forest line to Loughborough that same day.[36] The report said the boat carried 'nearly ten tons'; characteristically, a later account stated that the load was nearly twenty tons, and was pulled by two horses and six or seven men.

Not unnaturally, the company made much of the opening, and the entire town joined in the celebrations. The *Leicester Herald* turned with relief from reporting 'The empty pursuits of ambition and political folly' to give a lengthy account of the arrival of the first boats and the accompanying ceremonies, which it found 'infinitely more solid and fascinating'. The *Journal* went one better by transcribing an ode of vast length written and recited by Mr Coltman, a committee member, which listed all the good things to be expected from the new navigation: not only coal, iron, lead, lime from Barrow and (he hoped) Gracedieu and Barrow Hill on the Forest line, stone, and Swithland slate, but goods from further afield – indigo from Bewdley, deal, mahogany and other woods, millstones, merchandise from London, ale from Nottingham and Burton, 'rich suits, our wives and daughters to adorn' from Manchester, and 'such numerous things not easy to believe' from Birmingham. What with the extension at that moment being carried out by the Union company and the 'sister Navigation' to Melton also in progress, he said, 'from ev'ry quarter goods come floating in, We know not where to start or where begin'. Reading Coltman's effusion today, it is difficult to imagine that it added to the gaiety of the event, although it was 'frequently applauded' by its hearers. He had, however, been a most active worker for the project (apparently visiting nearly every house in the town to canvas for support): he had earned his brief spell in the limelight.[37]

It was indeed a festive occasion. Preliminaries began the previous night (Sunday), when two boats left Loughborough for Leicester. The following morning, about 11 a.m., the committee of the Leicester Navigation Company 'with many respectable Inhabitants', assembled at the Three Crowns Inn and walked in procession to the Public Wharf, the committee having provided 'flags and a band of music' for the occasion, reaching the wharf in time to greet the boats as they arrived. Symbolically, one of the boats contained coal from Coleorton, the other from Derbyshire. The committee boarded the Coleorton boat, and the chairman, Deakin, made 'an elegant and impressive speech' pointing out the blessings to be anticipated from inland navigations, especially this one. Coltman then pronounced his ode, after which both boats, with the committee and band aboard, continued along the navigation to the basin of the Union Canal near West Bridge, three cheers being given as the boats passed under each bridge. No doubt the rest of the throng followed along the towpath, for at West Bridge a 'very numerous' procession was formed, which proceeded through the streets to the Three Crowns, where the inevitable 'elegant entertainment' had been provided for over fifty committee members and guests, who spent the rest of the day in conviviality. No doubt diners would have agreed with the *Gentleman's Magazine* that 'the utility of (the navigation's) object has never yet, nor perhaps ever will be, equalled in the social and domestic history of this town', and they were probably right.[38]

CHAPTER 3

Setbacks and Successes

Difficulties and a new Act

The opening of the Forest line was purely a demonstration to enable the company to observe the letter of the law and open their main line for coal traffic. There was no immediate trade on the Forest line – or at least if there was, it passed free of toll, for Gildart, who had been appointed toll collector, was soon moved to the main line. He was installed at Mountsorrel to replace Middleton, the temporary man there; the committee had no doubt woken up to the fact that the trade in Mountsorrel

Junction of the Barrow Hill and Thringstone Bridge branches near Osgathorpe. The photograph is taken from the Thringstone Bridge branch; Barrow Hill branch enters from the left. The toll-collector's house can just be seen in the background

granite was likely to justify a toll collector there rather than at Barrow. Gildart continued at Mountsorrel until May 1795, when he was moved back to the Forest line, as the Leicestershire coalfield began to show signs of life. He was succeeded at Mountsorrel by William Robotham, at a salary of £20 a year.

There were the inevitable troubles in operating the line, some of which still cause concern to waterways officials today: children were playing dangerously near the water's edge (though the first recorded drowning was of a boatman), and the vandals, who are evidently always with us, damaged the brickwork of several bridges.[1] An example was made of a boatman who left his boat in a lock in the charge of two boys, who allowed it to hit and damage the bottom gates; he was fined £1 (it could have been much more) and put his mark to a public declaration of contrition.[2] In addition, attempts were made to cheat the company by declaring much less cargo than was actually carried. But these upsets were more than counterbalanced by the evidence of increasing trade – coal merchants were calling for better accommodation on the Public Wharf, and Staveley was ordered to produce plans for offices, which he duly did on 5 December. Shortly afterwards, building plots were made available adjoining the basin, but these were for sale only to those undertaking to trade by way of the navigation, and strict control was exercised over the design of the buildings. The tolls collected by Swinburne at Loughborough for the previous month had risen to £100. Northbound traffic on the other hand was still very small, having produced not quite £12 in the same month.

At the half-yearly General Meeting on 5 January 1795, the company took stock of their position. They had so far spent £69,630, including £187 10s. (£187.50) they had borrowed from the treasurers, and still had to raise more.[3] To go to their proprietors again was out of the question, especially as some had overcommitted themselves and were unable to pay even their current liabilities – Dr Bree, for example, who had done so much for the project, now owed £280 on calls on his shares – which, it is pleasant to add, Carter, one of the treasurers, said he would pay. The proprietors of seven shares still refused to pay the extra £30, and two new £100 shares had to be created and sold to the treasurers at £5 premium to make good the deficit. At least one of the proprietors was incensed at being wrongly accused of being in arrears and threatened with forfeiture. The company therefore accepted the offer of their treasurers to lend them £1,500 at 5 per cent interest, and agreed to try to raise a further £1,500 from elsewhere on the same terms.

An additional source of worry arose in connection with the Forest line, which, passing through empty countryside and with few of the company's servants at hand, was an obvious target for vandalism. Staveley reported 'considerable damages' in the Shepshed and Coleorton areas, and indeed there seems to have been a deliberate attempt to sabotage the line, for a coal carrier named Daniel Smith was given fourteen days imprisonment for throwing stones and rubble into the water.[4]

An ominous portent was the flooding which struck the navigation in February 1795, closing it for several weeks.[5] The works throughout were nearing completion, aided by a further loan from both treasurers, but work on the Forest line fell away to such an extent that Orchard, the superintendent, had his pay cut to 15s. (75p) a week. No doubt he had been relieved of some of his responsibility when Gildart returned to the toll-house at the junction on the Forest line. The chairman and two of the committee went in person to watch a cargo of coal worked over the Forest line in the company's own boat.[6] But clearly the committee

Toll-collector's house at the junction of the Forest line at Osgathorpe

pinned its faith on the River line, for on 10 April the committee members asked the Loughborough company to delay a closure for repairs so that Leicester could be fully stocked with coal before traffic was interrupted on the Loughborough navigation. By the beginning of May, Leicester seems to have amassed its stockpile, for there were over 500 tons of Shipley coal alone (on sale at 9d. per cwt) at the Shipley wharf, in Pasture Lane.[7] Shortly after this, the company itself acquired a stockpile and unwillingly entered the coal trade. Burslem, of Coleorton collieries, told the committee that he could not continue without assistance, since, it would seem, the Forest line was still incapable of taking coal in quantity. The committee felt that it was essential to keep the Coleorton pits going until the completion of the waterway and railways eased the transport problem, and they therefore agreed to advance up to £20 a week to Burslem, in return for which he was to deliver coal to them, to the value of the advance and at the rate of 8s. (40p) per ton, on their land adjoining the canal at Thringstone Bridge. When the Forest line was usable, Burslem was to buy back the coal at the same rate. They began with an advance of £40, some of which was recovered during the year, for by 28 August Gildart had sold £20 worth of it. Coal continued to be delivered, and by late October Gildart had raised a further £137 from sales. The committee was anxious that this arrangement should not last long, and called for a report on the line from Jessop, who duly replied that the trouble was leakage, which could be stopped by puddling. Water would still be short, he said, and work should be pushed ahead – he admitted that the reservoir would probably leak too, but not significantly.[8] This put the committee in a difficult position, for there was no money to pay for the reservoir, and their borrowing powers were exhausted. However, backed by the knowledge that trading activity was increasing and their tonnage returns looked reasonably healthy, they boldly recommended to the General Meeting on 6 July 1795 that the money should be raised by calling on all proprietors to pay £5 a share as their portion of the reservoir's cost, and this was accepted. Moreover, it was ordered that money arising from the tolls should be applied to carrying on the works.[9]

On 17 July 1795, Staveley was ordered to make a plan, specification and estimate of the proposed reservoir, and produce it at the committee meeting on 24 July, which he did. The works were quite heavy, the embankment for the reservoir head being about 14 yd high and 120 yd long. The contract was duly advertised in three local and two national newspapers. Several firms tendered, and the contract was eventually awarded on 7 August 1795 to a local man, John Clark of Fleckney, at £1523. But he then thought better of it, and backed out, being released from the contract on 17 August. The committee had had enough of contractors by now, and decided to do the work by direct labour, under Jessop and Staveley.

By the end of the year, £619 had been spent on the new reservoir out of the £1,730 advanced for the purpose. The committee, however, was still short of money for completing the works already in operation, and even after raiding the reservoir fund for £104, they were forced to ask the General Meeting held on 4 January 1796 to allow them to borrow up to £3,000 to liquidate the company's principal debts and to carry on the works; permission was duly forthcoming. Meanwhile, the growth of traffic on the River line was giving rise to operational difficulties. The channel itself needed attention, and the committee ordered Staveley to get a dredging boat built for this. At the same time, neglect on the part of some of the riparian owners was causing trouble – the miller at Sileby, for instance, was told to repair the bank at once. Boatmen were causing annoyance by unloading their cargoes while in locks, or on to the towpath, causing delay and obstruction, and the General Meeting passed a bylaw forbidding the practice.[10] One of the navigation's biggest users, Coleman, Ella and Co, protested at this, but the committee was firm. The first capture under the bylaw was a boatman who loaded 10 quarters of beans while in Mountsorrel lock. Another was charged with failing to draw the 'cloughs' of the lower gates of Cossington lock after he had passed through. Difficulties were also arising in the gauging (assessing the amount of cargo on laden boats) and the advice of the toll collector at Trent lock, on the Erewash Canal, was sought.

The same assembly, concerned by the slow rate at which tonnages were increasing compared to operational costs, tried to make some economies, such as reducing the salary attached to the clerkship from 80 to 60 guineas a year (£84 to £63), the post being combined with the supervision of the general legal affairs of the company and carried out by Carter and Cardale. They also considered the general financial position of the company. To date, the navigation had cost £76,654 while tonnage receipts to 26 October were £3,949. The General Meeting concluded that the tonnage rates authorized by their Act had been set too low, and decided that an Act to amend them was desirable. As the traders would obviously object to paying more, one of the committee members, Prest, was sent to talk the Nottinghamshire and Derbyshire coalowners into agreeing.

Forest-line work was advanced enough for the committee to order milestones to be set up, but by early April 1796 they had decided that there was no likelihood of traffic along it for the time being, and they therefore dismissed Gildart the toll collector, with effect from midsummer.[11] Lords Stamford and Moira were also canvassed, together with a number of other prominent coalowners in west Leicestershire. What the committee said to them is not recorded, but no doubt they stressed the amount that the company had already spent, the numerous works still unfinished, the debts unpaid and how their income from the tolls for the first half of 1796 was only £1,730.[12] It must have been with great relief that the committee learnt that the influential Lord Moira had agreed to support them, and the General Meeting of 4 July 1796 resolved that application should be made to Parliament for powers to borrow up to £30,000 to liquidate their debts and to raise the tonnage rates on coal between Loughborough and Leicester.[13] A subcommittee reported on the necessary amendments to the original Act which would be required for the new one, and drafted the petition to Parliament. Some difficulty was experienced with the Leicestershire and Northamptonshire Union Canal Company, who demanded that the increased tolls should not apply to coal passing along their line beyond St Mary's mill (about a mile south of their junction with the Leicester Navigation). The Leicester refused, and sent their chairman and clerk to London to lobby MPs about it. Feeling in Leicester was against them, too; even the usually friendly *Leicester Journal* thought it was premature to raise the tolls before a fair trial of the old rates had taken place.[14]

The LNU, on reflection, and in view of their far from happy financial position, were prepared to be bought off, and invited the Leicester to make proposals. After careful thought the Leicester proposed that, whenever they were in a position to pay a 6 per cent dividend without taking the increased toll on traffic to the LNU or the Melton, then all vessels passing on to the LNU and going further south than St Mary's mill should be free of the increase.[15] The LNU's Leicester committee, however, would not even call their Harborough equivalent into consultation on these terms, saying that it was a waste of time, upon which the Leicester amended its offer to make it apply when the dividend was 5 per cent and the point beyond which the increase should not be demanded Aylestone mill (a mile or so south of St Mary's mill). The LNU agreed to consider this.[15] Their General Committee eventually approved the offer, subject to the capital on which 5 per cent dividend was to be paid being limited to £92,000, to the Leicester sending copies

(1043)

ANNO TRICESIMO SEPTIMO

Georgii III. Regis.

CAP. LI.

An Act for enabling the Company of Proprietors of the *Leicester* Navigation to finish and complete their several Works, and to discharge the Debts contracted in the making thereof; and for amending an Act passed in the Thirty-first Year of the Reign of His present Majesty, for making the said Navigation, and several other Works in such Act mentioned.

[3d *May* 1797.]

Preamble recites Act 31 *Geo.* III, Cap. 65.

WHEREAS, by an Act passed in the Thirty-first Year of the Reign of His present Majesty, intituled, *An Act for making and maintaining a Navigable Communication between the* Loughborough *Canal and the Town of* Leicester, *and for making and maintaining a Communication by Railways or Stone Roads, and Water Levels, from several Places and Mines to the said* Loughborough *Canal, and for continuing the same, by passing along the said Canal to the said Navigable Communication, all in the County of* Leicester; certain Persons therein named, and their Successors, Executors, Administrators, or Assigns, incorporated by the Stile of *The Company of Proprietors of the Leicester Navigation*, are authorized to make a Navigable Communication for Boats, Barges, and other Vessels, between the *Loughborough* Canal and the Town of *Leicester*, by making certain Cuts or Canals, and by rendering the Rivers *Soar* and *Wreake* navigable

3 12 H 2 in

First page of the amending Act of 1797 for the Leicester Navigation of their half yearly accounts to the LNU, and to the LNU being allowed to examine the Leicester's account books and have any enquiries answered twice a year. All these conditions were accepted by the Leicester. Negotiations with the Melton were conducted separately.[17]

Other parties tried to get something for themselves out of the proposed Act. William Pochin of Barkby was advised to ask the company to put in clauses compelling them to make sundry culverts, weirs, etc. to prevent damage to his lands; naturally the committee demurred, but eventually gave way. The trustees of the Wanlip turnpike road, a short, little-used affair linking the Leicester–Loughborough and Leicester–Melton roads, were, however, unsuccessful in their attempts to get compensation clauses similar to those the company had been forced to put into their original Act for the Ashby and Whitwick roads. The company might well have pointed out that, far from taking traffic off the Wanlip road, the navigation must have created a good deal of new traffic to and from Barkby wharf, which lay at the point where the road crossed the cut from the Wreake to the Soar. The Oakham and the Melton Navigations were arguing their case with the Leicester representatives in London. The latter wanted to take an extra 3d. per ton on coal from the Leicester passing on to the Melton but not going on to the Oakham, for which 1d. was to be given to the Melton, while coal passing through Melton and on to the Oakham was not to pay any additional toll, and the committee gave them *carte blanche* to settle as best they could.[18] All these difficulties were resolved without much trouble, and on 3 May 1797 the company's new Act received the Royal Assent.

The Act (37 Geo III, c 51) began by stating the current position. The proprietors, the Act announced, had nearly finished the works, but had spent their authorized maximum of £66,000 and contracted debts of nearly £14,000 above this. They were therefore empowered by the Act to raise a further sum not exceeding £18,000 (nearly this sum had in fact already been raised), each proprietor advancing a sum in proportion to the amount of his holding; but an Ordinary or Special General Meeting of the company could opt to raise all or part of the £18,000 by mortgaging the tolls, or by granting annuities from the tolls, provided the sum raised was not less than £2,000. The money advanced by some of the proprietors for making the reservoir in Charnwood Forest, now nearly complete, was to be taken as part of this £18,000 and 5 per cent interest was to be paid upon money advanced for the reservoir account until the time of the first call made under the present Act.

The canal had, the Act declared, cost more to make than expected, and to compensate for this, the tonnage rates were to be raised: coal passing the whole length of the navigation from Loughborough to Lady's Bridge or West Bridge in Leicester was to pay 6d. (2½p) per ton, that to intermediate places ½d. per ton per mile – but coal passing on to the Melton Navigation was to pay 3d. per ton. The exemption negotiated with the Leicestershire & Northamptonshire Union was then spelled out, while coal passing on to the Oakham was also to be exempt from the increased rates. Finally there were clauses compelling the company to increase the flow of water to Hudson's channel at Wanlip by way of the Thurmaston weir and to protect Pochin's lands at Barkby.

The committee were not slow to avail themselves of the powers of their new Act, and decreed that the new rates should come into force on 15 May. At the same time, they did not neglect the obligations the Act placed them under to Hudson, and ordered that work should begin on altering the weir at Thurmaston forthwith. Trade now looked very promising. John Beaumont built lime-kilns for burning the product of the Barrow-on-Soar quarries at Syston, Thurmaston, and Leicester, as well as on the Melton at Rearsby.[19] An attempt was made soon afterwards to build up a passenger and light merchandise trade when one Pearson of Basford got the committee's consent to put a 'passage boat' to work on the line, paying a tonnage of £1 per voyage each way, no more than 10 tons of goods to be carried.[20] Pearson seems to have done little further for a time, but early in 1798 he announced that his 'packet boat' would be ready to enter service on about 20 February, with a passenger fare of 5s. (25p) for 'the Gentlemen's Room' and 2s. 6d. (12½p) for 'the Common Room for other Passengers'. Goods would be carried for 1s. (5p) per cwt. Departure from Nottingham was at 8 a.m., and the boat was to arrive in Leicester between 4 and 5 p.m. It would return to Nottingham on the next day but one.[21] But Pearson's enterprise was not rewarded. As early as 9 March 1798, he appealed to the committee for a reduction of the tonnage to 10s. (50p) per trip, which they seem to have granted.[22] Even at this rate, the venture did not pay, and on 21 December, Pearson announced that owing to lack of support 'and the Tonnage being so high on the Leicester Navigation', he was obliged to give up.[23] The General Meeting on 7 January 1799 offered to reduce the rate between 10 October and the following 5 April each year to 5s. (25p) per trip.[24] Pearson's reaction to this is not recorded, but it is likely that he withdrew from the field, for on 22 March 1799 John Maddock announced in the *Leicester Journal* that he was introducing 'Nottingham and Leicester Packets' on 25 March: a boat, with Maddock personally supervising the comfort of the passengers, was to leave the Navigation Inn, Nottingham, at 7 a.m. on that day for Leicester, returning at 8 a.m. on the following day. The service thenceforth would be Nottingham to Leicester every Monday and Thursday, returning on Tuesday and Friday. Passengers could get 'Tea, Coffee, Ale, Porter, Eating, etc.' on board.

The first call authorized by the new Act was made at the General Meeting on 3 July 1797. It was for £10 per share, though to offset this, £5 plus interest was to be returned to those who had advanced money for making the new reservoir. At the same time, the committee was authorized to borrow £8,000 to liquidate the company's debts, and to reduce tolls on the Forest line in order to induce the still reluctant Leicestershire coalowners to use it. Deteriorating economic conditions, no doubt emphasized by the proprietors' exasperation at the frequent demands for more money, resulted in the call raising only £1,001, less than a third of the anticipated sum. The committee had to make frantic efforts, and to threaten many of their proprietors with forfeiture of their shares, to get the arrears in. They had some success, ultimately raising nearly £3,230, although such prominent shareholders as Sir Charles Grave Hudson and Edward Miller Mundy held out long after most had paid up. They were able to set to work clearing up numerous small debts, leaving larger ones for future settlement, as in the case of the £2,630 they owed their clerk, Carter, which, having borrowed a further sum from him to bring the total up to £3,000 they left outstanding at 5 per cent interest.

The toll reduction on the Forest line was ratified by a Special General Meeting on 25 September 1798: from 10 October, coal from the pits at Swannington, Coleorton, Thringstone, Breedon, and Gracedieu was to pay 2d. per ton for its journey over the railways to Thringstone Basin; thence to Loughborough, all coal was to pay 10d. per ton, or 1d. per ton per mile in the case of coal stopping short of Loughborough. It is unlikely, however, that the Forest line had contributed much to the improvement of the company's finances that the committee were able to report to the General Meeting on 1 January 1799. In particular, tonnages were up, at £2,556, and in view of this, a maiden dividend was declared of £3 10s. (£3.50) on the 502 £140 shares, and £2 15s. (£2.75) on the 9 £100 shares. The holders of the latter were offered the opportunity of bringing them up to parity with the £140 shares by paying the £30 difference, but they did not do so, and this handful of awkwardly-priced shares remained to vex the company's financial agents throughout the

Mountsorrel granite wharf

rest of their history, though their number was reduced to seven on 8 February 1799, when the treasurers agreed to raise the two £110 shares they held to £140; later, two more £110 shares were sold and raised to £140, leaving five at the £110 figure.

The committee were actively engaged in developing trade on the main line, and negotiating with the Leicestershire coalowners to get them to use the Forest line. On the main line, they were exploring the possibility of developing business in commodities other than coal – Mountsorrel granite, gypsum and lime in particular; they actually helped a trio of traders to establish a bank of lime-kilns north of the Public Wharf in Leicester, in which Crich and Barrow limestone was being burned by June 1798.[25] On the Forest line, they agreed that, as the railway to Coleorton wanted extending, the company would give Sir George Beaumont 200 yd of cast-iron rails. They also agreed to a demand by Beaumont's agent that they should restrict the toll on the line to a maximum of 1s. (5p) per ton from Coleorton to Loughborough for at least ten years, and not charge tonnage on the weight of the wagons, either going loaded to Loughborough or returning empty. From this it seems that wagons were being carried on the boats to avoid transshipment, as suggested years before.[26]

At long last, there were signs of activity among the Leicestershire coal-owners, as notices announcing the sale of coal from Thringstone Green and Coleorton collieries appeared in the press.[27] Coleorton coal must have passed along the railways at the western end of the water level and along the water level itself, for it was sold at Loughborough Lane End at 9s. (45p) per ton or 5½d. per cwt. The Thringstone coal, at 3½d per cwt, must have been sold near the pithead. In Loughborough itself, hopes of trade on the line rose, boats auctioned there in January being noted as specially suitable for this purpose.[28] Tonnage figures for the whole navigation rose to nearly £3,000 for the second half year of 1798, and William Robotham, at Mountsorrel toll-house, was given a pay rise to £45 per annum on account of the extra work he was doing.

Disaster on the Forest line

The year 1799, which had opened so promisingly, suddenly became disastrous for the company. The *Leicester Journal* told the story succinctly:

> On Tuesday last [19 February] a most unfortunate and distressing circumstance occurred on the forest line of the Leicester Canal, near Sheepshead. In consequence of the thaw, the water swell'd so rapidly in the Reservoir, as to occasion the middle part of the head for about thirty yards, the aqueduct, and large embankment, to give way; the violence of the water carried away in its progress the whole of Chester's house and premises, a small house near Blackbrook, several stacks of hay and corn, about 50 head of sheep, and the fences and roads are torn up, and the land injur'd to an extent of near six miles: happily no lives were lost.[29]

Staveley's report to the committee confirmed this, adding that another house near to Chester's had been completely destroyed and that great damage had been done to the water level.[30] Jessop was called in, and his report, with estimates of £3,466 for repairs and £2,727 for damages was considered by the committee on 5 April and sent by them to a Special General Meeting on 8 April, which authorized them to get restoration work done 'forthwith'. Jessop laid the blame on 'the want of sufficient capacity in the discharging weir at the Head of the Reservoir' which caused the level of water to rise until it flowed over the top of the head, when it quickly made a breach by which the whole of the 870,000 tons of water were discharged. The passage under the aqueduct, though 16 ft wide and 18 ft high, was insufficient to take the onrush of water, which rose to a height of 30 ft for 300 yd along the embankment – the latter being broken down almost to ground level in places. Jessop could see nothing wrong with the construction of the head – if it had been a foot higher, it would have contained the water – although he suggested that the weir might be lengthened from 9 to 13 yd and lowered 2 ft, and the head should be raised 2 ft.[31] The committee, in adopting the report, recommended that an 'able Engineer', preferably James Barnes, who had served the LNU in a similar way in connection with the trouble they experienced in building Saddington tunnel, should be asked to survey the Forest line and report whether it could get sufficient water (from coalmines and other sources) to dispense with the reservoir altogether, or, if not, to say whether it would be better to build a new reservoir on a different site rather than patch up the present one.

The catastrophe naturally caused widespread local concern – not only to the sixty-eight occupiers of lands directly injured by the flood, of whom Joseph Chester was by far the greatest sufferer, his damages amounting to £1,105 out of a total of £2,767. One account says that the burst, which happened at about 11 a.m., only moments after the men watching the rise of the water level had left the head, emptied the reservoir within eleven minutes, and, apart from breaking down the embankment taking the canal over the Blackbrook valley, did considerable damage to the main Loughborough to Derby road. The latter became impassable, though next day forty men were at work clearing it, no doubt hindered by the crowds of sightseers which poured in.[32]

The committee at once set about getting the wreck of their reservoir and water level tidied up, so confidently that even before work began they wrote to Fenton and Raper and Boultbee asking them to press ahead with the opening of their new pits, in order to be ready when the line reopened.[33] But the coalowners' interest in the line had once more waned, and the sole result was an offer from Fenton, which was declined, to lease a colliery to the company. Sufferers from the flood got a first payment of 10s. (50p) in the pound early in June. Claims of less than £2 were paid in full. Despite their previous unfortunate experience with contract work, the committee decided to put the repair work out to tender, explaining that they wanted the work doing 'with as much Dispatch as may be'. Tenders were examined on 7 June 1799, but perhaps the committee realized that they had been too hasty, for Barnes had accepted their invitation to survey the damage but had not yet reported. He did this at the next meeting, on 21 June, and, estimating the cost of repair at £1,123, offered to get the work done by a 'proper Person' at this price. The committee agreed, and on 1 July 1799, made a contract by which Barnes, in association with Thomas Peake, undertook to reinstate the embankment, aqueduct and water level, and another by which he was to restore the reservoir head – in this case, it would seem from later payments, using Samuel Townley Blundell as his agent.[34] The committee also appointed an assistant to Staveley in connection with the repair work. They also took advantage of the availability of such an eminent engineer as Barnes to get him to look at the lands in the Barkby area which had been covered by the clause for the protection of Pochin in their 1797 Act, and which had been flooded at the same time as the reservoir had burst. Barne's recommendations were accepted, and Staveley was asked to get the work done.

Barnes and his colleagues pushed ahead energetically, the greater part of the work being done by the end of the year. After this, there was a marked slackening, and even by the end of October 1800, the work was not completed, for Barnes then wrote asking for settlement of his account, with deductions for incompleteness. In fact the deduction was only £20 in the case of the reservoir, while the embankment appears to have been finished.

But once again disaster had struck. On the night of 25 March 1800, water leaked through the puddled bottom of the water level on or near the aqueduct, and eventually brought down part of the structure, including a wing wall. The committee suspected sabotage, and offered a reward for information leading to the conviction of the hypothetical miscreants who had bored holes in the puddle.[35] There is no evidence that they were right; certainly nobody ever claimed the twenty guineas. John Crossley, in 1834, attributed the second failure to bad workmanship.[36]

On 2 May, the committee, whose dogged determination to get traffic moving along the Forest line can only be admired, and who certainly did not deserve the calumny cast on them later that the Forest line was a mere gimmick in which they were not interested, wrote yet again to the coalowners telling them that the line was likely to be ready for trade within a month. The missive was greeted by stony silence from the coalowners, and both sides appear to have shelved the matter for over a year. Then the committee, no doubt despairing of persuading the coalowners to use the line, accepted an offer by Douglass, a Loughborough millowner, of £30 for one year for part of the water of the line for his mill. Clearly the aqueduct had not yet been rebuilt, for the committee agreed to pay half the cost of bringing water over the breach at Blackbrook. The agreement was to be cancelled 'in case' the water level was reopened. This aroused Beaumont's agent, who said that the Forest line was so 'very imperfect and out of repair' that he could not recommend Beaumont to connect his present works with it; but the committee retorted that as soon as Beaumont showed any signs of wanting to use the line, they would put it in order. The arrangement to supply Douglass with water went ahead, and, attempts to repair the breach having failed, Douglass had a 'trunk' put across it at his own expense, Staveley supervising the work.

At the beginning of 1803, the committee once more took the matter of the Forest line in hand. They had clearly decided that the hybrid canal-cum-railway nature of the line was a serious drawback, and resolved to call in an engineer to report on the possibility of making a canal to link the water level with the main line of the navigation in Loughborough. Sensibly, they got the best man possible: Thomas Telford, who, at a special committee meeting on 4 January, was instructed to report on the best way of altering the line so as to improve it for the transport of west Leicestershire coal and lime.[37] Telford duly reported, and, by invitation of the committee, John Braithwaite came to discuss his report as representative of Fenton and Raper of the Swannington colliery area. He was not encouraging. Collieries in that area had mostly closed, and would not be reopened unless the company reduced its tonnage rates and guaranteed a sale of 20,000 tons a year. The committee were as accommodating as possible, saying that they were ready to put the canal, railways, and reservoir into repair if Fenton and Raper and Beaumont would undertake to send coal in quantities of that order. But the matter got no further. It may be that Telford's report proposed nothing better than the existing line, in which the coalowners had no faith – this seems to be supported by the wording of a committee minute which refers to putting 'the Canal, Reservoir, and Railways into repair for Use as originally intended by Mr Jessop and approved by Mr Telford.'.

It is quite evident that the committee were by now losing heart, and the Forest line disappears from their records for a long period. They even neglected to pay Telford for his report for over two years; he was finally voted it as a belated Christmas present on 26 December 1806.

That they were turning from trying to develop the line towards merely making it safe is clear, for in 1804 they tried to get Barnes to come down, in view of the failure of the reservoir, to see that the water was discharged through the head. But Barnes, too, had lost interest, and Staveley was given the task of making the necessary aperture in the reservoir head instead. It was the final admission of defeat.[38]

Among the legacies of trouble the committee inherited from the section of the 1791 Act dealing with the Forest line were the clauses relating to compensation to be paid to turnpike trusts controlling roads which expected to lose trade by the building of the line. One of these was the Whitwick to Markfield road. The committee soon came to doubt whether this road ever had any coal trade to be harmed by their line. Still more did they suspect that the trustees were pocketing the payments made by the Leicester Navigation Company and neglecting to repair their road. In 1802, they ordered one of their clerks to study the position, but, as the compensation was a mere £3 10s. (£3.50), they took no further action. However, with the possibility of the line being developed, they evidently thought it best to get rid of a potential incubus, and commissioned Edward Parsons to survey the road and its traffic. Parsons' report was scathing: the road was 'intolerably bad' and had not been repaired for at least twelve years. Why there should be a turnpike road there at all he could not see, but if this one were to be continued, 'it ought to be Indicted from one end to another'. But the failure of their latest efforts to develop the line discouraged the committee from doing more than pointing this out to local MPs. Their chance came, however, in 1805, when the turnpike road trustees, perhaps stimulated by this severe criticism of their road, applied for an amending Act. By an adroit mixture of blandishments and threats, the committee persuaded the trustees to accept a lump sum instead of the annual guarantee, and for £125 were relieved of its burden.

The company's affairs improve

Despite setbacks on the Forest line and a trade recession in the early years of the nineteenth century, the company's affairs were looking up, tonnage returns showing a satisfactory increase in the volume of trade.

The growing volume of work unfortunately found some of the company's servants unsuited to their responsibilities. William Swinburne, the toll collector at Loughborough – and therefore holder of a key position – gave rise to dissatisfaction as early as 1798, probably for failing to send in his tonnage returns promptly. Later he was given permission to gauge boats passing on to the Loughborough Navigation on behalf of the latter, and for a time matters improved. In 1801, however, Swinburne was censured for irregularities in his accounts. These were quite trivial, but on 29 May 1801, the committee declared that boats passing down the navigation were not being assessed for tonnage accurately, especially those laden with wool. This was a serious matter, particularly as it implied that two of the company's servants – Swinburne again, and Robotham at Mountsorrel – were neglecting their duties; and both men were ordered to use their gauges to get accurate results. Swinburne was again in trouble in August of the same year, for failing to get satisfactory bills of lading from the masters of boats passing his office. But all was in vain. On 27 November 1801, the committee were informed of 'divers Instances of Misconduct and Neglect' on Swinburne's part, and summoned him to answer the charges. He failed to clear himself, especially of having neglected to pay to the treasurers a considerable part of the money he had received. (There are indications that this was due not to dishonesty, but to giving boatmen credit for their tolls.) Be that as it may, he was dismissed on 14 December. The gravity with which the situation was viewed by the committee is shown by the fact that the matter was decided in three separate minutes, each of which was signed by all ten committee members present. William Robotham was to take over Swinburne's post temporarily, a permanent successor, Benjamin Gabb, being appointed on 26 December. A somewhat embarrassing situation followed for Swinburne refused to vacate the toll-house in Loughborough. The committee had already ordered the door between the toll-house and the toll-office to be blocked up, and Robotham to use only the outside door, but they now had to get an ejectment order to remove Swinburne, at the same time using a mild form of blackmail, offering him certain payments if he would go quietly. These manoeuvres succeeded, and no further trouble was experienced with Swinburne, although in the following year, his son plagued the committee with repeated demands for payment, all of which were rejected, for improvements to the toll-house carried out by Swinburne senior.

The toll collectorship at Loughborough at this time was evidently not an attractive position, for Gabb only remained there until December 1804, when he asked the committee to release him in three months, or less if possible. His successor, William Ferneley, was the Melton Navigation's toll collector at the junction of their navigation and the

Leicester. The company were unlucky in that just before this another toll collectorship had fallen vacant, on the death of Robotham of Mountsorrel. Fortunately, an adequate replacement was at hand in his son, and William Robotham was appointed to his late father's position on 7 January 1805.

While still preoccupied with the Forest line, the committee were trying to develop facilities on the Public Wharf to attract traffic. They were unable to increase the area of land they held there, the price demanded by the owner for the Leyroes (which adjoined the wharf)

The two Chamber floors to be of Inch & ½ Deals roughly plained and the joints plow'd & tongued.—

Two Stair cases strongly timbered, steps Inch & ½ deal with proper hand rails &c.—

Ten strong door frames 7 feet by 5 ft 6 ins. with Oak Sills, and foulding doors of Inch & ½ deals with proper fastenings. and well painted.—

42 Window frames 3 feet 6 inches Square with Oak Sills, and Whole deal Slides and Slats, with fasten-ings and well painted.—

A Gangway and other matter necessary for fixing a Windlass &c. in the Roof to be paid for Extra—

Christr. Staveley 18th April 1801.

Part of Christopher Staveley's specification for a warehouse at Leicester, 1801 being too high, but on 24 February 1801 they ordered Staveley to produce plans for a warehouse, 60 ft by 25 ft and three storeys high. Staveley did this, but a trade recession caused the committee to countermand their decision to build and it was not until 1804 that the project was taken up again. Even so, Staveley's project was too ambitious and a scaled-down version, capable of development when need arose, was authorized instead. The building was done by William Bradley and E. Morton at a contract price of £738. In connection with this building, a new basin was made, the work being carried out by William Read for £270.[39] Basin and warehouse were in use by 17 January 1806, by which time the committee had ordered a crane to be built on the wharf to serve it, and others inside the warehouse itself. Its management was entrusted to the company's wharfinger, George Webb, who received a pay rise of £25 for the extra work.

The Leicester Navigation and the millers

Of all the tribulations which beset the committee after the final failure of the Forest-line scheme, the most persistent came from the millers on the main line. There were ten mills between Loughborough and West

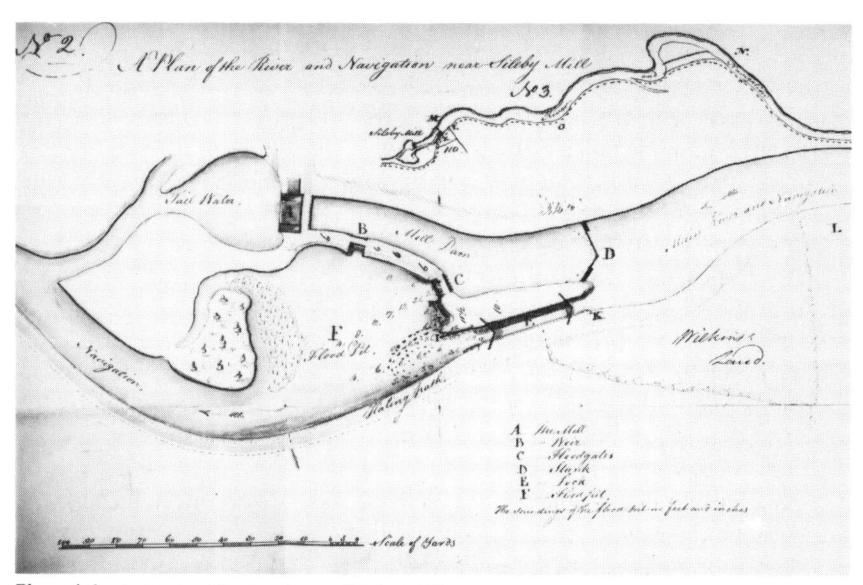

Plan of the Leicester Navigation at Sileby Mill, 1805

Bridge (Loughborough Lower and Upper, Barrow, Mountsorrel, Sileby, Cossington, Thurmaston, Birstall, Belgrave, and North), and it is safe to say that the company had trouble with every one of them at some time – as was to be expected, for the purposes of the two sides were incompatible, and the best that could be hoped for was an uneasy compromise which might be upset at any time. Usually the millers acted independently of one another, but on occasion they united to make joint demands – as in 1800, when they demanded compensation for water shortage in June and July, and 1806, when they asked the company to amend the compensation payments. The committee refused the 1806 requests and the matter was settled by the arbitration of Neale, of the Melton Navigation, who awarded a total of £86 9s. 9d. (£86.49) to the millers.

Sometimes millers took matters into their own hands. In 1802, John Kirke of Cossington mill (a paper mill at the time), being impatient at the committee's delay in reassessing his compensation, seems to have helped himself to one of the company's towpath gates in part payment, and hung it as a gate to his garden instead. An indignant committee got a warrant for his arrest, but as Kirke had put in a claim for damages and got the commissioners appointed under the 1791 Act summoned to investigate, honours were about even, and the matter was smoothed over.

Disputes were usually settled less drastically. At Mountsorrel, the committee made a grant of £22.10s. (£22.50) towards rebuilding the waterwheel, in return for which the miller agreed that they should no longer be liable for loss of water unless it were drawn off specifically on the company's instructions. But mills were a constant source of concern, and the committee's decision in 1801 to bid up to £1,000 to buy Barrow mill for the company is understandable, though their valuation proved to be hopelessly out – the mill was sold for £2,000 (the new owner promptly asked the committee to pay for alterations to it, which, as he refused any quid pro quo, they declined to do). The sale price of Barrow mill serves to show what substantial vested interests these navigational obstacles could be, and in some cases difficulties were increased by their owners being men of greater influence – Thurmaston mill, for instance, belonged to the Earl of Stamford.

Easily the most serious dispute with a miller, and one which cost the company dear, was that which arose between them and the Sileby miller, John Wilkins, in 1806. The company's case was that Wilkins was bound by the 1791 Act to keep his flood-gate in repair. He did not do

Sileby mill and lock on the Leicester Navigation

this, so that on 3 May 1805 it gave way, and so much water ran to waste that not a single boat could get through the navigation. For twenty-six days Wilkins made no attempt to repair the flood-gate and the company's engineer eventually patched up a repair by putting in a stank. Wilkins subsequently repaired the gate 'at his leisure' but flatly refused to pay compensation. The matter came before Lord Ellenborough at the Assizes on 6 August 1806, the damage being assessed at £1,000. The case was then passed on to three arbitrators, who found Wilkins not guilty, blaming the Navigation company for placing the lock too near the flood-gate and thus putting excessive pressure on it. The arbitrators also claimed that the lock had been made 'in an improper manner' and that by deviating two watercourses the company had undermined the wing walls to the flood-gate. This was in flat defiance of Jessop's evidence; both he and Staveley asserted that the decayed state of the flood-gate was to blame and this was confirmed by the Mountsorrel miller. Wilkins was awarded £129 damages and £76 costs.[40] The verdict, given by a trio of Leicestershire landowners in the teeth of evidence presented by the company's expert witnesses, must have been a bitter pill for the committee to swallow. They took legal advice from several sources as to the advisability of appealing, but received no encouragement. There was nothing to do but pay up – and, apart from the damages awarded to

Wilkins, solicitors' bills cost £299. All they could do was to instruct Staveley to keep a watchful eye in future on all the flood-gates on the line, especially at Sileby; a necessary precaution, as the latter was in bad repair again by March 1807.

Eventually, on the advice of Sale, the Grand Junction's clerk, the committee called in Benjamin Bevan, engineer of the Grand Union Canal, to submit a detailed report on the mills. His report, dated 21 June 1820, necessitated a supplement, as the committee did not understand it, and there was a further report on 13 December.[41] All were carefully thought out documents, characteristic of the judicious Bevan, making such points as that traffic passing along the Leicestershire and Northamptonshire Union to the Leicester brought water with it, and so should not pay compensation to millers. The average amount mills should be paid was worked out, and showed a striking variation, ranging from £11 for Thurmaston to no less than £75 for Barrow. The latter figure Bevan attributed to the great depth of Barrow lock, and he recommended making a side pond there, to be used only when water was short. Further correspondence shows that he regarded 2s. (10p) an hour as a reasonable payment for stoppage of mills, but he adds that the Soar could not be relied on to provide even twelve hours a day working in summer, and that the company should not be expected to pay compensation for stoppages they did not cause. The committee offered terms to the millowners based on this report, and no doubt because of Bevan's reasonable findings, had little trouble in persuading the millers to accept them.[42] In the following year, the committee made a further effort to save water and reduce compensation payments by enforcing, from late summer, the practice of 'waiting turns' (a boat going uphill through a lock was not to pass until a boat had come downhill through it and vice versa, even if this involved waiting for a boat to come along from the opposite direction). In the second half of 1821, however, millers' compensation payments still totalled £355, thus swallowing up more than the whole of the company's warehouse profits and rents of £331. As time went on, the mills' importance declined, and one by one they ceased work. Some, however, survived into the twentieth century and continued to draw their annual payments from the Leicester Navigation Company. Mountsorrel, for instance, received payments until 1915, and Cossington to 1931, while three of the mills were paid up to the time when the company went out of existence: these were Birstall, Sileby and Cotes (Loughborough), the last payments to them being £3, £6 5s. (£6.25) and £17 10s. (£17.50) respectively.

CHAPTER 4

Monopoly and Competition

Traffic on the Leicester Navigation in the early days

The register of boats imposed by the Act of 35 Geo III (1795), compelling all boats of more than 13 tons burthen to be registered with the clerks of the peace of the counties in which their normal routes lay, is especially interesting in connection with the Leicester Navigation, coming as it does so soon after its opening. The returns are classified according to each boat's usual run. By far the greater number of those using the Leicester were registered as plying on 'the Navigation from Leicester to Cromford', though this description of course included the whole of the Loughborough and Erewash as well. There were thirty-seven of these, of which thirty-one were of 40 tons burthen, five of 35 tons, and one of 30 tons. Crews are given as two men, and the usual formula for a two-man boat runs 'to assist in steering and 1 (sometimes given as 'a boy') to drive the horse'. Often it is unclear whether this included the boat's master, whose name was recorded separately. One of the 40 tonners claimed to have a one-man crew, his job being to drive the horse; an obvious impossibility if there were not an extra man, clearly the master, to steer the boat. After the Leicester to Cromford the most popular run was from Leicester to Gainsborough on the Trent. The number of boats registered for this was six, all 40 tonners with big crews – four assistants to the master and one to drive the horse. Next came 'the Navigation from Melton-Mowbray to the Erewash and Cromford Canals' (though the Melton was not yet opened as far as the town) with five boats of 40 tons burthen, all with two-men crews – again, the master being understood as the third crew member. Four boats were registered for the run from Leicester to the Erewash, only one being a 40 tonner – the others were two 35 tonners and one 32 tonner. The short length of the Leicestershire and Northamptonshire Union so far opened had three boats registered as using it, the northern terminal being the Cromford Canal; two were 40 tonners, the other a 30 tonner. A solitary boat, of 40 tons, recorded its run as being from Leicester to Shardlow, at the southern end of the Trent and Mersey Canal.[1]

Trade 1797–1850

To the surprise of the proprietors, trade on the Leicester Navigation did not at once justify the perhaps extravagant hopes expressed over the years. The company blamed this on their maximum permitted tolls being set lower than was economically reasonable, and they may have had grounds for this, for the first full year after the amending Act of 1797, raised the tolls, and during the following year the tonnage receipts increased greatly. In 1796 they were £3,225, while in 1798 they were no less than £5,550. From then on tonnage receipts rose, but not continuously: indeed the committee became seriously worried when an exceptionally high figure of £6,867 in 1800 was followed by £6,327 in 1801 and £5,945 in 1802. This was, however, a temporary decline, and the general trend was upwards until the end of the Napoleonic War in 1815, when the figure was £9,615. Then followed a two-year slump, but recovery was rapid, and in 1820 for the first time the company earned a five-figure income from its traffic – £10,934. The next few years were the Leicester Navigation's golden age, the pinnacle being in 1825, when the tonnage returns were no less than £14,736 – the highest in the company's history. Although nothing like this was ever attained again, earnings were very handsome for the next eight years, only once falling below £10,000 and usually being well up in the £11,000 to £12,000 range. Then came a foretaste of future woes. The Leicester and Swannington Railway was partly opened in 1832, wholly in 1833, but the pits it was designed to serve were not in full production, nor was the railway's stock adequate to cope with great volumes of traffic, so the coal arriving in Leicester by rail did not at first affect the Leicester Navigation. But by 1834 this had changed, and Leicestershire coal began for the first time seriously to compete with the waterborne Derbyshire coal. The consequence was a sharp drop in the Leicester's tonnage receipts for the next two years – to £8,539 in 1834 and £7,676 in 1835. But a recovery began after this, no doubt due to rising demand in Leicester itself and the diversion of some of the Leicestershire coal south along the Union Canals, and receipts did not fall below £10,000 for the next three years.

Then, however, came a dramatic decline. In 1840 the Midland Counties Railway opened its line from Nottingham and Derby by way of Leicester to Rugby on the London and Birmingham Railway. The section of line planned to serve the Erewash valley coalfield area had been forced out of the Bill by political pressures, but the new railway immediately affected the Leicester Navigation's revenue disastrously. In 1840, the company's tonnage receipts fell to £8,000, and in 1841, the first whole year of the railway's operation, the figure was £6,943. There was a slight recovery in the railway mania years of 1845–7, the figure in 1847 rising as high as £7,983, but the ensuing slump was even greater: in 1849, the tonnages amounted to only £4,535, in 1851 £3,984, and in 1853 £2,583. Though there was a very slight recovery from 1857 (when the Midland Railway's new line ate into the Market Harborough traffic) the company never again earned as much as £3,000 in tonnages in any year; indeed, from 1874 the figure fell below £2,000 and stayed there.

Coal

Of the various commodities carried along the Leicester Navigation, coal was, as expected, by far the most important, and a brief survey of coal rates and prices during this period is instructive, since it shows very clearly the emphasis laid on the most profitable handling of coal. The survey also shows the uneasy relationships which existed between the canals of the Leicester line, an important point, as it helps to explain why the resistance of the navigation companies to railway encroachment on their traffic collapsed so swiftly and completely.

Throughout the period, suspicion of its neighbours, especially the Loughborough and Erewash companies, and of the coalowners, characterized the Leicester's attitude. As early as 1802, they refused to dispense with the additional tolls the Leicester was empowered to take from the Leicestershire & Northamptonshire Union by the 1797 Act, when that struggling company appealed for help, unless the Loughborough and Erewash lowered their tolls and the Derbyshire coalowners cut their pithead prices. Nor would they lower their tolls to get traffic moving along the Leicester line on the completion of the last link in the chain, the Grand Union, in 1814.[2] Even in 1830, when the projected Leicester and Swannington Railway threatened competition, the committee remained adamant: rejecting two appeals by William Jessop, son of the Leicester's first engineer and a leading Derbyshire coalowner, although Jessop had offered to reduce the pithead price of his coal by 1s. per ton and the other companies on the line had agreed to lower their tolls. The indifference, or blindness, of the committee to potential railway opposition is extraordinary: when in 1831 they were at length persuaded to lower tolls on coal passing over the Leicester line to the Grand Junction, by granting a drawback (rebate) of 3d. per ton, it was because of the competition of Staffordshire coal, not of railways.

But they were learning. In 1832, the first section of the L & SR was opened, and the threat of railway-carried coal entering the Leicester market became a reality: a trainload of coal was brought from the pits at Bagworth even before the line officially opened. Moreover, it was probably widely known that the Derbyshire coalowners were contemplating making a railway of their own to fight the newcomer, and this would inevitably cream off the Leicester's traffic. It is likely that this plan was communicated to delegates from the Loughborough, Erewash and Leicester at a meeting with the coalowners' representatives at Loughborough on 15 August 1832. The three canal companies agreed that each would lower its tolls on coal by one third, though this was not to exceed 6d. (2½p) or to apply to coal passing on to the Melton. The coalowners were not particularly satisfied with this, and must have been even less so when the Leicester committee subsequently restricted the reduction to coal sold in Leicester at 10s. (50p) a ton or less; the better quality Derbyshire coals fetched considerably more.[3] Nothing further was done until, in consequence of an increasing quantity of Leicestershire coal selling in Leicester at prices well below the Derbyshire product, coal merchants in Leicester made representations to the committee.[4] The latter replied that they 'had no objection' to combining with the Loughborough and Erewash in a reduction of 1s. (5p) per ton, if the Derbyshire coalowners would reduce their price. Subsequently they added that this reduction must be at least 1s. per ton, and must be passed on to the customer. Opinion among the coalowners was divided; but the committee must have seen the weakness of their position, for in the end, they granted the reduction unconditionally.

Railway competition became stiffer as the Leicestershire coal output grew, and as a result of L & SR toll reductions, cuts were necessary in the price of Derbyshire coal in Leicester, so that in 1834 the price ranged from 10s. (50p) per ton for Hallam, through 13s. (65p) for Old Shipley, to 15s. (75p) for Swanwick. These prices had changed little by 1838.[5] Leicestershire coal prices ranged from 8s. 6d. (42½p) for Ibstock to 11s.

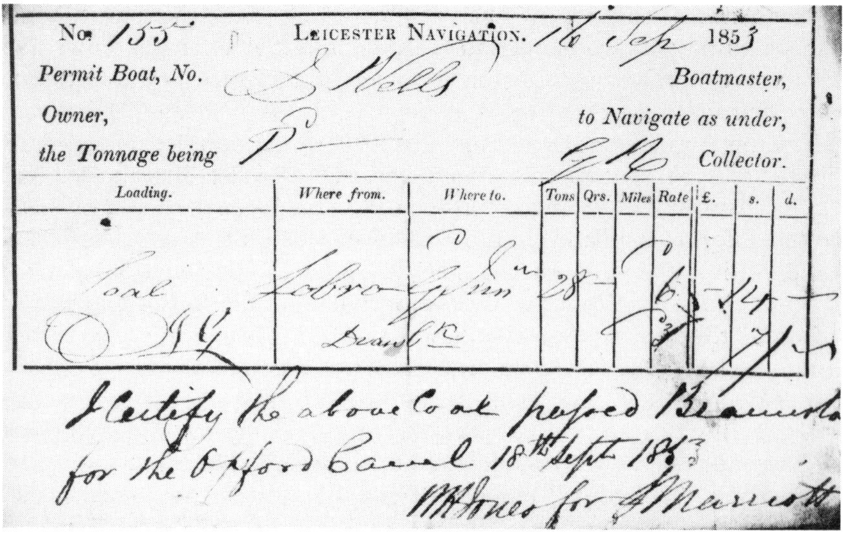

Return tonnage check of 1853 from the Leicester Navigation showing coal passing from Loughborough to the Oxford Canal via the Grand Junction

(55p) for Snibston and Peggs Green. A new competitor entered the field when, with the completion of the Coleorton Railway in 1834, Coleorton coal became available at 9s. (45p) per ton.[6]

The L & SR also made a bid for the Market Harborough coal trade, by offering a 6d. (2½p) reduction in tonnage rates or 'drawback' on coal bound for that town. The disunity between the canal companies was again obvious. The Leicester, calculating that a reduction of 1s. 7d. (8p) per ton was necessary to save the traffic, lowered its toll to 7d., expecting its two northern neighbours to do the same. But the Loughborough and the Erewash only knocked 5d. each off the tolls, whereupon the Leicester committee indignantly raised their toll to 8d. They were saved from thus cutting off their noses to spite their faces by the Loughborough's agreement to lower tolls proportionally, upon which the Leicester's toll was reduced to 7d. again. On two other occasions, in 1837 and 1838, the Leicester, though ready to make reductions, refused because the Loughborough and Erewash would not reciprocate. On the second, the Leicester thought that they were being asked to make a proportionally greater reduction than the Loughborough and Erewash. But a committee inspection of the navigation immediately after this upset brought them down to earth – no doubt traders on the line, and the evidence of half-empty wharves and warehouses, convinced them that something drastic needed to be done, and they offered a drawback of 4d. on coal to the Grand Junction even adding that they would not raise their toll if the coalowners made a slight price increase. There was still some juggling with figures. In 1839 the committee felt strong enough to increase the toll on coal to Leicester to no less than 1s. 3d. per ton, perhaps to make as much profit as possible before a second railway invasion, for the Midland Counties Railway was under construction; but more sensible counsels prevailed, and the toll was lowered to 8d. almost at once, and set at 7d. for coal passing right through to Paddington.

In 1840 the committee had an unpleasant foretaste of things to come when, with the MCR line through Leicester about to open, one of the most important carrying companies of the Leicester line, James Sutton and Co., announced that they were giving up their boats in favour of carrying between Leicester and the north by rail.[7] The following year, another of the Leicester's large carriers, Wheatcroft's, threatened to do the same if tolls on merchandise were not reduced.[8] With the bottom falling out of their world, the committee held discussions with other companies on the line, and of their own accord suggested that the Leicester's tonnage on coal to Paddington should be 4d. – a figure they would have scornfully rejected a few years before. In 1844, the L & SR and MCR having lowered their rates, the committee cut the Leicester's local coal rates by 6d. (2½p) per ton without waiting to see what anybody else on the line did. The Loughborough and Erewash followed this realistic lead, but were still not ready to go to the lengths the more farsighted were already planning, for they refused the Leicesters' suggestion that all coal along the line should pay the same cheap rate as that to Paddington. Even when it became known that the great canal carriers Pickford's were planning to abandon canals for railways, the Loughborough and Erewash still would not reduce their tolls further.

Through traffic in coal suffered immediately, but the development of railway depots at intermediate points was also cutting into the canal's trade. Kirke, the miller, boatbuilder, and wharfinger at Mountsorrel, and Ward of Barrow, both approached the committee asking for reduced tolls, as their trade had been greatly injured by the new railway wharves constructed at Sileby and Barrow by the Midland Railway, as the former Midland Counties Railway had become when it amalgamated with the North Midland and Birmingham and Derby Junction Railways in 1844. The committee agreed, granting a reduction from 5d. to 3d. on coal from

Loughborough to Mountsorrel, and from 4d. to 2d. from Loughborough to Barrow.

To what depths the company had been reduced in a few years was shown in 1849, when the committee gave the General Assembly the results of negotiations for their share of the Grand Junction's boatage fee on coal to London. With their tonnages lower than at any time since the 1797 amending Act and with the Loughborough and Erewash canals refusing to cooperate, the committee had been forced to allow the Grand Junction to negotiate first the two northern canals' share in the 6s. 10d. a ton fee, then to give the Leicester as much as they could afford of the remainder. In other words they would have to take what was left over when the other three companies had helped themselves. The Leicester company, thus humbled, had at least woken to bleak reality.[9]

Other trade

While coal was the mainstay of the company's finances, a wide variety of goods passed along the navigation. Lime was among the most important of these, prepared from two main sources of limestone, one at Barrow-on-Soar, close by the navigation, the other at Crich on the Cromford Canal. Barrow lime was greatly appreciated for its quality and seems to have been sold at about the same price as Crich despite the greater distance the latter had to travel; in 1820, both were on offer in Leicester at 17s. (85p) per ton. The stone was carried to Leicester and burnt in kilns near the Public Wharf – there were at least seven of these there by 1820.[10] Near them were kilns for burning gypsum for plaster (much of the stone came from near Syston, hard by the navigation) and the smoke and fumes eventually became a public nuisance – to such an extent that on one occasion the parishioners of St Margaret's began an action to stop it. The navigation also suffered: an accident to a boat in 1816 was caused by the steerer being unable to see because of the dense clouds of smoke from the kilns blowing across the waterway.[11]

Two other local industries were aided by the Leicester Navigation. The first was the quarrying of Mountsorrel granite, a very hard igneous rock highly suitable for roadmaking. So rapidly did this develop with the coming of the navigation that the inhabitants of Mountsorrel went to law to try to prove that the quarries were rapidly and illegally encroaching on their common land. They failed to convince the court. From 1818 onwards, orders for cargoes of this stone were regularly placed by the main Leicestershire turnpike roads, and a trade in 'setts' or blocks for

Mountsorrel granite wharf, *c.* 1890. Note the quarry and the windmill in the background

street paving grew up which extended from London to Manchester. The second local product encouraged by the navigation was Swithland slate, which apart from its obvious use as a roofing material, was also used to make a wide variety of articles, from cheese presses and sinks to chimney pieces and tomb stones. There were at least two wharves in Leicester devoted exclusively to slate – almost wholly Swithland, for, though Welsh slate was being sold in Leicester as early as 1803, its price must have made it uncompetitive.[12]

A survey of traffic on the navigation at a time when it was flourishing will indicate the variety of goods using it. During the period 24 June–10 July 1809, when the navigation was at its busiest, the Loughborough toll collector recorded the passage of 163 boats travelling south: sixty-nine of these were heading for Leicester, and a further fifty-three would continue on to the Leicestershire & Northamptonshire Union, twenty-three of these to the latter's terminal at Debdale wharf (the extension to Market Harborough not yet being open), and seventeen to Blaby. Of those terminating short of Leicester, sixteen were for the Melton Navigation, nine for the wharf in Loughborough by the Nottingham road, five for Barrow, one for Sileby, two for Mountsorrel, two for Cossington, two for Barkby (where the Wanlip–Syston turnpike road crossed the navigation) and four for Thurmaston. No fewer than 133 boats carried coal and three coke, four carried lime, and there were one each of 'stone' (limestone), flagstone, slate, lead, and iron rods, and seventeen boats laden with merchandise. The average cargo was 35–9 tons, but one of the boats travelling to Blaby bore 42 tons, and there were two others with 41 tons. In the same period, the Mountsorrel toll collector had to deal with thirty-five boats, nine of which came from the Melton Navigation, while twelve originated at Mountsorrel itself, and ten at Barrow. The others were from Barkby, Cossington, Leicester and Loughborough. In this case, stone was the chief cargo – Mountsorrel granite and Barrow limestone – twenty of the boats having this cargo, though the returns do not distinguish between the two stones. Other cargoes were coal (five boats), timber, lime (three boats), skins, pelts, reeds, and wool (one of the chief back-cargoes from Melton). The Leicester toll collector's returns for this period are not available, but in the following fortnight he recorded twenty boats of which nine carried wool and three 'goods', in this case probably hosiery. This return is typical of this period, and shows clearly that coal was indeed the life blood of the Leicester Navigation, and that the bulk of the navigation's trade passed southwards.

The Leicester Navigation and the railways

As early as 1813, a contemporary stated roundly that if the Forest line had been made purely as a railway, 'it would have survived to this day'.[13] The idea of a railway to link the Leicestershire coalfield and Leicester thus implanted by Jessop's mongrel remained dormant for years, but reappeared in 1826, when the *Leicester Chronicle* suggested such a line from the Ashby Wolds region.[14] The committee's only concern with the long dismissed notion of railways, however, seems to have been to sell off their surplus rail track, which, in November 1824 they ordered Staveley to advertise. They only succeeded in selling 25 tons, leaving 200 tons on their hands. William Fenton eventually bought 34 tons at approximately £10 per ton. The rest were still in store in 1831, when some were stolen from Thringstone.

The first moves towards a revival of the Leicestershire coalfield, which had never recovered from the invasion of Notts-Derbyshire coal brought about by the opening of the Leicester Navigation, came in 1827. At

Whitwick, a trio of Leicester men headed by the energetic William Stinson sank two shafts and by 1828 had reached a 6 ft-thick seam of good coal. Meanwhile, discoveries of coal were made at Ibstock and, after a year's prospecting, at Bagworth. The *Leicester Chronicle*, reporting this, expressed the hope that a railway could be built to develop new finds. Perhaps this was inspired by Stinson, whose name, wrongly spelled 'Stenson' and thereby causing him to be confused with a William Stenson who was employed by the Whitwick Company in a relatively subordinate position, is always traditionally associated with the origins of what was to become the Leicester and Swannington Railway. He must certainly have been anxious to establish a satisfactory means of transport between his Whitwick colliery and Leicester, while elsewhere in the coalfield production was increasing: demand far exceeded supply at Ibstock, a new colliery was opened at Alton Grange, another at Hugglescote, and the Coleorton pits, closed for forty years, were reopened.[15]

Despite the indications of activity in west Leicestershire, the Leicester Navigation company's committee seem to have been taken by surprise when, on 17 November 1829, they read a letter from John Cradock, clerk to the Loughborough Navigation, about a projected railway 'from Whitewick [*sic*] to Leicester', calling for a meeting of delegates from the Erewash, Loughborough and Leicester Navigations. The committee sent representatives, but the meeting decided nothing, and they seem to have been unable to make up their minds what to do; in the end, they called a Special General Meeting for 22 July 1830. Their position was weakened by the fact that at the time of the November meeting the navigation was closed by frost, and coal was coming by road at excessive prices – a matter which was seized on by the press, as anxious now to get a railway to Leicester as they had once been to get a canal.[16] The Special General Meeting authorized the committee to take such steps as they thought necessary to get protective clauses in the Leicester and Swannington Railway Bill as it went through Parliament, and also seized the chance to ask Parliament to allow them to abandon 'this most useless and onerous burthen', the Forest line, and sell the land. Unfortunately, their first effort to get a clause inserted in the Bill failed, as standing orders were not complied with, but they succeeded in inserting a second clause, compelling the railway company to make basins so that boats could lie out of the fairway wherever trans-shipment wharves were sited.

The railway project was naturally causing the Derbyshire coalowners anxiety. Two of their leaders, Jessop and Barber, were ready to lower their pithead prices by 1s. (5p) per ton if the canal companies would reduce their tonnage, and they were certain that other coalowners would follow their lead – they had to 'if they expect to sell any coal'.[17] The Erewash, Loughborough and Leicestershire & Northampton Union had agreed to this, but the Leicester committee rather feebly declared themselves legally unable to act without the assent of a Special General Meeting, which would take two months to summon. Worse still, Lord Stamford suddenly woke up to the fact that the Forest line, one purpose of which was to serve his limeworks at Cloud Hill, Breedon, was out of action, and peremptorily ordered it to be put into good order at once. The committee refused, leaving Lord Stamford to show good reason why such an expensive operation should be carried out.

No doubt they were at last realizing that the railway threat was a real one, for plans had been deposited for a railway from Cromford to Leicester that was likely to be far more damaging to them than the Leicester and Swannington, and they united with the Loughborough and the Erewash to oppose it. They were more ready to consider toll reductions now: the rate on coal passing over the Leicester line for the Grand Junction, reduced from 1s. 2d. to 11d. in 1819, was now lowered to 8d. per ton, and they thought that if other companies reduced their rates further, the Leicester should do the same. In order to give the committee speed of manoeuvre, they also asked the General Assembly to authorize them to vary tolls without calling a special meeting, and this was agreed. The committee speedily made use of their new powers to lower the coal tonnage by a further 2d. to 6d. (2½p) per ton on 2 January 1832.

In 1832, following a request by Sir George Beaumont's agent for the restoration of the Forest line and in view of the known interest of other proprietors along it, the committee decided to have the line surveyed. They therefore engaged W.A. Provis, who had collaborated with Telford for many years, to view the line. Provis's report, dated 27 June 1832, is a most interesting document. Discussing the railways, he said that the line was ruled out for locomotive traction by its gradients, which included 30 chains at 1 in 70 and 48 chains at 1 in 30 – the latter, in fact, he considered too steep for horses. The gradients could, however, be eased by encroaching on the canal, and would then be practical throughout for horses. The canal was in reasonably good order, and could be restored fairly cheaply. But he pointed out the drawbacks that accompanied the trans-shipment of goods, saying that although it would be possible to avoid these by carrying wagons on boats, this would greatly increase the working costs. So, he argued, either the Loughborough–Nanpantan railway must be made into a canal, or the canal must be converted into a railway. The former would be expensive to make and would require an Act, but the canal could be made into an effective railway cheaply by laying rails on the towpath; it would have to be horse-worked because some of the curves were too sharp for locomotives. Not much could be done about the railways to Coleorton and Swannington, as these had gradients of 1 in 24 and 1 in 26, but they might be replanned if business warranted it. The branch line to Barrow Hill, Osgathorpe, should, Provis said, be made (by implication, Lord Stamford should be left to make the Cloud Hill branch himself if he wished). The total cost of the work would be £18,256 plus £1,399 for the branch. The General Meeting of 2 July 1832 accepted the report, and authorized the committee to get the work done. They set to work at once getting counsel's opinion as to whether a fresh Act was necessary (it was) and writing to coalowners on the Forest line of their intentions. At the same time, they did not neglect traffic on their main line, and in an effort to conciliate the Derbyshire coalowners – already known to be contemplating a railway to counter the L & SR – agreed with the Loughborough and Erewash to a joint reduction of toll on coal, amounting to a total of 1s. 6d. (7½p).

Provis, called on for a final survey of the line, took the opportunity, since the company had to go to Parliament anyway, of making some improvements to the route, the total cost, for a single-track line with three 'turnouts' or passing places, now being £38,606, the line being 2 miles shorter than that of his original plan. Interest in the company's scheme was growing – a new independent railway was projected to join it to the L & SR at Swannington, Lord Stamford's agent wanted the same end to be achieved by an extension of the Forest line itself, and Stinson asked permission to make a branch railway from the Whitwick collieries to it. Charles March Phillips, of Garendon, objected to the line as 'an annoyance to his Estate', but everybody else seemed to welcome it. Everybody, that is, except the proprietors of the Leicester Navigation. The final estimate, after Provis had put in various amendments to appease Phillips, amounted to no less than £52,607, and this great difference from the original estimate was too much for them to stomach: the Special General Meeting of 24 December 1832, having heard a long and detailed account of the project, decided by the narrow majority of seventy-three to seventy not to proceed further with the matter.[18]

But the half-yearly General Meeting on 7 January 1833 thought otherwise, possibly because it heard that the committee had felt obliged to go along with the Erewash and Loughborough in a toll reduction on coal, which had the effect of reducing the company's income for the half year. The committee were therefore authorized to have surveys and estimates done for a railway from their main line to the coalfield. They were also told to oppose both the Bill for a line from Pinxton in the Erewash coalfield area to Leicester sponsored by the coalowners, and the L & SR's move to enable them to build a bridge over the navigation in Leicester to their proposed new coal wharf in Soar Lane. Another project which came before the committee was a line from the L & SR at Swannington to the Ashby Canal tramroad at Worthington, a scheme which ultimately materialized as the Coleorton Railway; they elected to remain neutral, perhaps because this line would at least free them from Lord Stamford's claims.

Provis had been too expensive, and the committee sought elsewhere for its new consultant. With their talent for selecting outstanding engineers, they picked James Urpath Rastrick, who visited the Forest line on 27/8 February 1833. While hampered by the lack of detailed plans, Rastrick saw no difficulty in converting the line to a railway, either horse- or locomotive-worked. He proposed to straighten the railway at the Loughborough end and make part of it, near Burley Wood, into a 1000-yd self-acting inclined plane. The horse would make the downward journey in a two-wheeled carriage at the rear of the train, eating its corn and getting strength for the return journey. For much of the water level, the company's ground could be used for the railway, the only major deviation being at Finney Hill, where a 220-yd tunnel would be made. There would be another 200-yd tunnel near Thringstone, and a 1000-yd self-acting incline (to Peggs Green) at the termination. As the committee were understandably anxious not to spend money on the branch to Swannington, he left it out. Assuming that a horse could make six journeys along the line in a day, haulage would cost 0.65d. per mile: a locomotive would do it for half that figure, but the tunnels would have to be made wider and higher for locomotives. The main line, single track with sixteen turnouts, would cost £38,841, and the branch to Barrow Hill £5,979. The cost of any land required was excluded.

For some reason, the committee decided to have another survey done, and commissioned Thomas Hill of Wakefield to carry this out. In many respects, Hill's findings were similar to Rastrick's – he devised an inclined plane from Loughborough to the water level, followed the latter very closely for most of its length, and made Peggs Green the object of his main line. He estimated that the total cost would be £19,082 (including a branch to Cloud Hill at £2,941). This was so much below previous estimates for railways in this area as to be suspect – the more so as the committee got an estimate of £35,944 from Samuel S. Harris for a railway on the line suggested by Provis from Loughborough to Peggs Green. Provis was recalled and asked to survey for a railway to be built 'at as little expense as possible'. The committee had now determined that they would abandon the Forest line and build a new railway from the coalfield to Loughborough, and on 5 November 1833, they recommended this to a Special General Meeting. Provis's report showed that he had completely re-thought the line. Originally, he said, he had planned to have the junction between the new railway and the Leicester Navigation 100 yd from the junction of the latter and the Loughborough Navigation, running thence south of the Loughborough's basin to take up the old line west of the Derby road, and he still thought this the best line. An alternative had been suggested which would run south of Loughborough town, but this would be more expensive. As the committee wanted as cheap a line as possible, he suggested that certain of his improvements could be cut out and added at a later date when finances permitted it; his revised estimate for the complete system of 13 miles 746 yd was therefore £31,850. The meeting accepted this, and authorized the committee to take the necessary steps to bring the matter before Parliament. This they did, but the Bill soon ran into trouble. There was a formidable list of petitions against it, including Lord Stamford's agent, who was being troublesome about restoring the Forest line again. Worst of all, Lord Shaftesbury, chairman of the House of Lords Committee, took exception to the company's privileged position with regard to the clause in their 1791 Act exempting them from paying poor rates on their tolls, and demanded that it should be abandoned (over the whole navigation, not just the Forest line) before the Bill could proceed. A Special General Meeting was called on 15 May 1834 to consider this, but naturally the proprietors could not agree to the proposal, and it was decided to withdraw the Bill completely.[19] This was not quite the end of the company's efforts to develop a share of trade in Leicestershire coal. The committee evidently concluded that Lord Stamford might have had a point in his agitation for a revival of the Forest line, and sent their engineer, Crossley, to report on the possibility of its restoration in the form devised by Jessop. Crossley examined the line thoroughly (though he failed to observe that the Cloud Hill branch had never been made) and concluded that the whole line could be restored at a cost of £20,245, and would return a revenue of £2,484 or 8 per cent on capital. The report went before the General Meeting, but no further action is recorded in connection with it. By way of a postscript, it may be recorded that one enterprising Leicester coal merchant, John Ellis, approached the committee for reduced rates for coal from Leicester to Loughborough, with a view to L & SR-borne coal competing with the Derbyshire product there. The committee were helpful but there was little future in this trade.

By now the Leicester no longer had the matter of railways in west Leicestershire to itself. Loughborough interests, seeing the failure of the company's schemes and having heard no further word of the Pinxton–Leicester railway, promoted by the Notts–Derbyshire coalowners, promoted two railway schemes, one from Swannington to Loughborough, the other from Swannington to Zouch on the Loughborough Navigation. The engineer of the former was no less a person than George Stephenson, who, however, does not seem to have thought much of it, as he referred to it as 'of inferior importance' and not worth taking to Parliament if the landowners opposed (his interest in the line was as part owner of Snibston colliery, near Whitwick).[20] In fact, neither scheme got beyond the planning stage.

A far more serious threat to the Leicester's trade was the Pinxton to Leicester line itself, which, far from having died as the Loughborough people thought, had been transformed into a major trunk-line project, to serve Derby and Nottingham as well as the coalfield, linking them and Leicester with London by way of the London and Birmingham Railway, then under construction. Under its new title, the Midland Counties Railway, it was discussed at the General Meeting on 5 January 1835. Considering how long this project had been in the making, it is surprising how little of the committee's attention it had occupied, although the frequent negotiations with the Loughborough and Erewash to try to establish toll rates on coal satisfactory to everybody were no doubt largely activated by the knowledge that the railway scheme was there. The next reference to the MCR was on 4 January 1836, when the General Meeting authorized the committee to oppose the railway if it felt this best for the company. When the MCR's Bill came before Parliament, the Leicester, Erewash, and Loughborough united in demanding the removal from the scheme of the line serving the Pinxton district, i.e. the section running through the coalfield area. They were unsuccessful, but other, more influential, interests had the same idea, and when the MCR Act was passed, it had been shorn of the Pinxton section.[21]

It was during the first period of their brush with the railways that the company suffered a major scandal at the hands of their principal officer. Edward Staveley had succeeded his father as surveyor in 1825, and, to all appearances, had run the company's affairs ably and efficiently. On 9 April 1833, however, a hurriedly summoned special meeting of the committee was astonished to hear that their clerk, Halford Adcock, had been visited that morning by Brown, Staveley's legal representative. Staveley had instructed Brown to inform the company that he was deficient in his accounts to the tune of £1,400. The committee promptly dismissed Staveley, and ordered Brown to return all the company's books and papers – he evaded this for a time, however, and while they were arguing, Staveley bolted.[22] The committee got back the books, and with them they inherited Staveley's clerk, John Crossley, who was to serve them well in both engineering and administrative capacities, and later to achieve fame as the engineer of the Midland Railway's Bedford–London extension and Settle–Carlisle line. A warrant was taken out for Staveley's arrest, and a police officer was sent with it to Birmingham and Liverpool, but no trace of Staveley was found. All that could be ascertained was that he had fled overseas, leaving the company £750 poorer, and with a row on their hands with one of their treasurers, who had stopped from their account £500 which Staveley had pocketed. And thus ended dishonourably a connection with the Leicester Navigation going back to the earliest days of the project.

CHAPTER 5
Decline and Absorption

The Leicester Navigation after 1850

By 1850 the railway network was extensive and still increasing, and already the railways had a stranglehold on what had been the most lucrative parts of the Leicester line's trade. The companies of the line were crippled in their attempts to fight the new competition by their disunity, the canals at the northern end in particular being apparently unable to realize that the brave days of their transport domination had gone for ever, and also by their failure to produce the quality of leadership which could have ameliorated their plight if not avoided it. Only Thomas Grahame of the Grand Junction, and later of the Grand Union and Leicester & Northamptonshire Union, seems to have been farsighted enough to grasp that the line's one hope of salvation lay, not in fighting to recover traffic lost to the railways, but in developing new forms of traffic to replace what had gone. During the 1850s he put much effort into persuading the companies of the Leicester line to give concessions to encourage trade in livestock to the London market, even suggesting special types of boat to be built for the purpose.[1] The Leicester rather grudgingly allowed a toll reduction, but were clearly not very interested, and the business never developed. Indeed the only trade which *did* increase was that in nightsoil from the growing town of Leicester, which expanded to such an extent that at one time forty boats engaged in this malodorous trade passed along the navigation, which according to contemporary accounts they reduced to a most unsavoury state. The company also extended their interest in the licensed trade (they already owned a public house at West Bridge) by purchasing the Navigation Inn at Barrow-on-Soar for £200 in 1861; the inn remained the company's property until 1920, when they sold it for £650.

Despite those new interests the committee's sovereign remedy for their troubles was still alteration of the tonnage rates. They continued to

Barrow-on-Soar: Pilling's lock

think of coal as the mainstay, although they should have seen the danger signals – as, for instance, in 1852, when the Eastwood collieries flatly refused to pay a surcharge of 1d. per ton imposed in 1840. A further threat came in 1854, when the Midland Railway revived its intention to take up a scheme it had projected years before, for a line from near Leicester by way of Market Harborough to Bedford and Hitchin, and the Leicester followed the LNU in lowering their coal rates to Harborough by 1d. per ton. Eighteen fifty-four was indeed a bad year for the Leicester line. Through traffic in coal fell by 22,216 tons on the Leicester, and the Loughborough and Erewash put up their tonnage rates, taking the view that there was more hope of recouping their losses by imposing higher charges on what trade was left to them than of enticing some of the lost traffic back by lower tolls. The Leicester, to mark its disapproval of this step and persuade its northern neighbours to see reason, put up its own rates to the legal maximum. The move worked: a scale agreed on by a meeting of delegates of the Leicester line companies was accepted, the Leicester undertaking to accept 5d. per ton for coal passing the whole length of their line, whether the ultimate destination was Leicester or beyond. The Loughborough, however, took umbrage, and refused to lower their tolls, whereupon the Leicester put their rates back to the maximum. The Loughborough gave in, and reduced the tolls again, and the Leicester followed suit. All this took three months, during which time the unfortunate traders still using the line can hardly have known what rate they were supposed to be paying. It is small wonder that Old John Gill, the toll collector at Mountsorrel, chose to retire at this stage. He was succeeded by Thomas Carr, at £30 per annum. He, like many of the company's servants, stayed with them for a very long time, until his death in 1912 – upon which his widow took on the job, giving the Leicester the unusual distinction of having a lady toll collector.

There were a number of important changes among the officers at this period. John Crossley, honorary engineer since 1851, resigned in 1859. In 1860 Halford Adcock gave up the clerkship. The Loughborough toll collector, George Nash, died in 1861 and was replaced by Reuben Gilson at a salary of £70 per annum. The loss the committee evidently felt most deeply, however, was that of the Leicester agent, Henry Dawes, who died in 1862; they ordered that a headstone should be erected at the company's expense on his grave in Belgrave churchyard, where it can still be seen, commemorating his loyal service. His son, Charles James Dawes, took over his office, and began a remarkable career with the Leicester Navigation, for he held the post until 1901, and, on resigning, was elected to the committee, of which he soon became vice-chairman, remaining such until his death in 1923.

Toll alterations, with inter-company squabbles a usual concomitant, were the main feature of the next two decades. Occasionally the company was frightened into agreement by a sudden glimpse of reality – in 1860, for example, a proposed lowering of tolls on coal to Market Harborough and Northampton was abandoned because the Loughborough and Erewash thought that 'it was very desirable to prevent a collision with so powerful an opponent as the Midland (Railway) Company'.[2] But ringing the changes had little effect. The tonnage receipts fell from £4,968 in 1850 to £2,883 in 1860. The fall was less rapid in the 1860s, the return in 1869 being £2,408, but from 1878 it was pronounced again. In 1890, the figure was down to £980, and only twice after this did it again ever reach four figures. It was at this apparently unpropitious moment that the Grand Junction persuaded by the carrying firm of Fellows, Morton and Co. that the Leicester line was capable of winning far more trade than it had, set to work to seek it. The effort

Fellows Morton and Clayton wharf, *c.* 1900, on the Leicester Navigation

was completely unsuccessful, and indeed the year 1903 showed the lowest tonnages ever returned – £704.

The company made few developmental moves in this period: Thurmaston mill was bought for £1,300 in 1859, probably because of the compensation payments saved rather than for its trading prospects, and in 1869 Barrow mill became a plaster mill and was let at an increased rent of £140. Rather the story was one of the shedding of former assets which declining trade had turned into liabilities. In 1855, the expenditure on the company's West Bridge wharf was found to exceed receipts, so it was let to Charles Bowmar. In 1857, the post General Meeting dinners were abandoned. In 1869, land near the Public Wharf was sold as a site for St Mark's Church.[3] The Public Wharf itself shrank: some of it was leased to the Grand Junction, more was laid out as new streets and building plots, and part of the Lime-Kiln Wharf was leased to the borough as a nightsoil embarkation point. An issue which had caused trouble throughout the company's history, compensation paid to millers for loss of water caused by the passage of boats, was tackled in 1871. As

Barrow-on-Soar: the navigable cut is visible on the right and the river and mill on the left

far back as 1858, Thomas Wicksteed, summoned by the committee to report on watermills on the Leicester Navigation, had concluded that the company were paying through the nose for the loss suffered by these mills. The seven mills from North mill (Leicester) to Mountsorrel in 1857, for instance, had experienced damage to an amount Wicksteed calculated as £10 8s. 11d. (£10.45), whereas the compensation paid to them was £196 16s. 6d. (£196.82½). Since the number of boats using the navigation had declined greatly since then, it followed that even less water was being taken away from the mills, and the company therefore argued that their payments should be reduced. Most of the millers were amenable. The sum paid in 1871 was £273 16s. 6d. (£273.82½); this was reduced over the next few years, until by the 1880s it became £70 9s. (£70.45), which remained the standard figure for many years. The company were still paying compensation to the surviving mills down to the end of the company's independent life in 1931; only Birstall, Cossington, Sileby and Cotes survived into that period. Another regular payment which was standardized was towpath rents – at £60 per annum.

The company had money in hand from disposing of some of their assets, and in 1880 they decided to follow a course which also commended itself to their neighbours the LNU – to make a sum, in this case £4,000, available for borrowing on the security of freehold property.[4] By 1881, £3,800 was thus invested. This provided a fair income, to offset to some extent their declining returns from other sources – the lime-kiln rents reduced from £80 to £50 in 1882, the rent of Thurmaston mill from £40 to £30 in 1884, even the committee's own payment for attendance from £40 to £20 in the same year, and the clerk's salary from £63 to £42 per annum in 1889. Under the circumstances, it is hardly surprising that the committee should be interested when they learned that other parties were considering taking over their concern.

The Leicester Navigation and the Leicester Flood Works

Lying as it did on the banks of the sluggish River Soar, Leicester has long been subject to flooding. In 1672, for instance, at least one, possibly two, drownings occurred in a 'great flood' in the North Gate–West Bridge area.[5] The situation became worse as the town grew and land which had acted as a natural drain became covered by buildings. In 1853, with the town expanding very rapidly, the Local Board of Health for Leicester became seriously alarmed by the prospect of regular and damaging floods, and commissioned a report by the engineers for the two navigations which passed through the town, John Crossley of the Leicester Navigation and George Foxton of the LNU. The report, which was presented to the Local Board of Health on 8 December, made various recommendations which would have cost the modest sum of £2,024.

However, no action followed, but the problem did not solve itself, and the report was reprinted in 1861 and 1867, by which time the situation was such that Leicester Corporation went to Parliament for an Act (the Leicester Improvement, Drainage, and Markets Act) which they obtained in 1868. The clauses which affected the Leicester Navigation empowered the corporation to widen the navigation near the L & SR offices near West Bridge, to make a weir on the navigation near the Whitwick Dock, and a new cut from this weir to the Soar. Alterations to the main (unnavigable) course of the Soar through Leicester were authorized, and one of these, involving work between Swan's Nest weir and Belgrave mill, was the first part to be begun. This was not until 1873,

Thurcaston road bridge at Belgrave, 1905. The navigable channel is on the far left

however, and then mainly because of further serious flooding in the times in 1872) and because the corporation had bought Belgrave mill for £5,400 in 1872, acquiring with it considerable rights over the waters at this point. Even so, a plan drawn up by two eminent engineers, Hawksley and Hawkshaw, in 1869, for which the corporation paid £315, was quietly shelved when it was found that it would cost £130,370 to execute, and this did not include the price of land or compensation.

Galvanized into action by the flooding, the corporation obtained an Act in 1874 to allow a considerable extension of the flood works scheme. On the Leicester Navigation, a new lock was to be constructed near the Public Wharf, and the navigation between that lock and Belgrave mill was to be straightened and deepened, adopting an idea originally suggested by the Borough Surveyor, E.L. Stephens, several years before.[6] To meet the Leicester Navigation's objections to having its traffic interrupted – and perhaps permanently lost – while the new lock was being built, a channel was to be made from the navigation to the Soar at Abbey mill corner, so that boats could be diverted on to the Soar, picking up the normal line of navigation at Belgrave lock.[7] A new flood

Junction of the Leicester Navigation and Old Union Canal near West Bridge, Leicester, 1872

river was to be made from Swan's Nest weir to Belgrave mill (this necessitated the rebuilding of the weir), and while this work was in progress the corporation decided to incorporate a new lock in it, to replace the one at Belgrave mill. They did not put the work out to tender, but had the contractors for the weir, Benton and Woodiwiss, carry it out at an estimated price of £1,700; it was completed by 27 April 1880.[8]

Work was begun, but 1875 proved to be a disastrous year, the town being subjected to four separate inundations – in one, Belgrave Road was under three feet of water, and in another, two canal boats near West Bridge were so violently banged together by the torrent that one sank.[9] In consequence, another Act, the Leicester Improvement Act 1876, was obtained, sanctioning work on streams associated with the Leicester Navigation to carry off flood water more quickly. This work was carried out slowly, as the corporation were concentrating on operations in the West Bridge area, but a large number of men having been thrown out of work by the severe winter of 1878–9, the corporation, as a relief measure, began clearing the Willow Brook, in the vicinity of the Public

An old print of Belgrave mill on the Leicester Navigation

Wharf. They also succeeded in coming to an arrangement with Hitchcock, owner of the North mill, giving them his water rights for £8,060, and in making agreements with other factory owners which enabled them to let the whole of the flood works on the main channel of the Soar from North Bridge to Belgrave mill as one contract, awarded to Benton and Woodiwiss of Derby for £32,376, of which about £6,500 was chargeable to a fund instituted for the creation of a public park between the Soar and the Navigation.

Operations on the lower district (West Bridge to Belgrave) proceeded slowly, as the corporation were now considering more extensive works above this, and were negotiating for the purchase of Swan's mill (eventually acquired in 1880 for £18,000). Plans for the lowering of the navigation between the Public Wharf and the Swan's Nest weir were ready by 30 April 1878, but no attempt was made to get the work done.[10] In 1879, however, the town was given a further reminder of the urgency of the flood problem when, after heavy rain, there was bad flooding in the Belgrave Road area, aggravated by the blocking of the Willow Brook by contractors' equipment being used to deepen it.[11] Even worse were the floods the following July – in fact, these were the worst since 1852 – when the water between Dorset Street and the Melton Road was so deep that tramcars had to give up running – whereas the Abbey Meadow, hitherto regularly inundated, was quite free of water, which was carried off by the new flood channel.[12] There were further floods in September and October, and in the latter some of the new flood works were damaged.[13] Work on the Willow Brook was stopped fifteen times in eight months at this point, sometimes for a week at a time. The corporation at once ordered its flood works engineer, Frederick Griffith, who had taken charge of the works on 1 March 1879, to report and, when the report was received, they submitted it to Hawskley for his opinion. That being favourable, and negotiations with the various interests involved being completed satisfactorily, they went to Parliament for an Act which was passed as the Leicester Improvement Act 1881. The most important clauses of this related to the Leicestershire and Northamptonshire Union, but the Leicester was affected: the section between North lock and the junction with the LNU was to be deepened and widened, and the fall of North lock was to be reduced.

North lock, Leicester, on the Leicester Navigation in 1908

So far, the works in the lower district had concerned the Soar, but on 17 February 1881, the contract for widening and deepening the Leicester Navigation from the Public Wharf to Swan's Nest weir was let to Whittaker Brothers of Horsforth, near Leeds, for £9,234. The associated works on the Willow Brook were let in July to Bryan W. Ward for £1,906. The contract for the work above this was not let until later: on 27 March 1883, that for the navigation and the Soar from Soar Lane to North lock and North Bridge respectively were let to Kellett and Bentley for £13,700 while the contract for the works to Soar Lane Bridge and Bow Bridge went on 5 September 1883 to S.W. Pilling and Co. of Manchester, for £27,990.[14] The work on the North lock appears to have been entrusted to Whittaker's, who finished it on 3 August 1882, when they were paid £344 for it.

The works, let piecemeal, were finished likewise. Benton and Woodiwiss had virtually finished their contract on the Soar from Swan's Nest weir to North mill by 29 March 1881, and had been paid £41,094 (which included the new lock at Belgrave). Whittaker's had nearly finished the new lock (Lime-Kiln lock) by the Public Wharf at the end of June, and completed their contract by 26 October, having been paid £11,111, the excess being due to extra works.[15] Traffic had been diverted from the normal line on the Soar along the temporary cut linking the two from early April 1881 to, probably, August.

The Leicester Navigation at the turn of the century

One of the results of the Railway and Canal Traffic Act of 1888 was that the Leicester Navigation, in common with other canal companies, was required to furnish details of its undertaking, and these are available for several years. The first are for 1888 itself. The waterway was said to be capable of taking boats whose maximum dimensions were 70 ft long, 14 ft 6 in wide, and 3 ft 6 in in draught. Paid-up capital was £76,150, out of a total of £84,000 authorized. Traffic on the line in this year amounted to 95,843 tons, none of which was carried by the company. The revenue was £2,392, of which £1,170 came from tolls. The total expenditure, including maintenance of the works, was £1,140, so that if the company had relied on tolls alone for its income, it would have made a loss. Most of the boats using the navigation were horse drawn, but there were occasional steamboats. All eleven locks were said to be 90 ft long and 14 ft 6 in wide. The depth of water on the sill at Mountsorrel and Barrow locks was given as 3 ft 7 in and 3 ft 11 in respectively, all the rest being 4 ft 6 in.

Dredger at Mountsorrel lock on the Leicester Navigations, *c.* 1890

The 1894 returns under the Railway and Canal Traffic Act are still more helpful in portraying activities on the Leicester, for they give a detailed breakdown of traffic which shows that coal now brought in only £384 against £641 from general merchandise. The coal traffic, though not large, seems to have been fairly constant in the 1890s, which were lean years for the Leicester: in 1890, coal passing along the navigation to Leicester amounted to 13,652 tons; in 1891, 12,769 tons; and in 1892, 13,828 tons. The once all-important through traffic in coal had virtually disappeared: only 115 tons were carried over the Leicester on the way to London in 1890. The trade in Mountsorrel granite and Barrow limestone remained important, no less than 35,609 tons being carried in 1890. A trade which had arisen with the establishment of a gas company in Leicester was that in gas by-products, and this formed an important element in the local traffic on the Leicester Navigation : 12,285 tons out of a total local trade of 15,829 tons in 1890; 10,421 tons out of 13,244 tons in 1891; and 9,568 tons out of 12,525 tons in 1892. The company was in fact anxious to put up the tolls on this last traffic. They had not altered any of their rates since 1873, coal, for instance, still paying ½d. per ton for the first mile from the junction with the Loughborough (to encourage trade to wharves on the Leicester Navigation in Loughborough) up to 4d. per ton for the whole length. Merchandise paid 6d. per ton for 9 miles or more. Limestone was charged, not by the ton, but 18s. (90p) per boatload, which was normally 47 or 48 tons. Mountsorrel granite was charged 3d. per ton to or beyond Leicester, 2d. to Loughborough.

The returns for 1898 give even more welcome details of the traffic, which totalled 94,038 tons. Of this, 26,517 tons passed through the canal from outside sources to destinations beyond the Leicester; 29,003 tons came on to the navigation from outside for unloading on the line of the Leicester; and 16,635 tons were loaded on the navigation for destinations elsewhere. Thus, well over one-third of the traffic was of local origin. The revenue was £2,326, tolls contributing £1,043 (not much more than rents, which produced £979). Expenditure was £1,053, of which £692 went on maintenance and £313 on management. Curiously, the locks had apparently shrunk in the preceding ten years, the uniform 90 ft of the 1888 returns giving way to figures varying from 84 ft 6 in for North lock to 88 ft 6 in for Lime-Kiln and Belgrave locks; this may have been due to taking internal instead of external measurements, or to rough-and-ready methods in 1888, perhaps by measuring the nearest lock and assuming that all the others were the same. The fact that, as might have been expected, the two newest locks were also the biggest (they are 15 ft 6 in wide against the 15 ft 0 in of the others) also confirms belief in the greater reliability of the 1898 returns generally. The falls of the individual locks do not agree in the returns of 1888 and 1898 either – the difference being as much as a foot in the case of North lock. The 1905 measurements confirm those of 1898 exactly.

The 1905 traffic figures show that 82,551 tons passed along the canal. Of this, 24,936 were through traffic; 26,684 tons came from outside for delivery on the Leicester Navigation; 16,704 tons were loaded and discharged on the navigation, and 14,227 tons were loaded on the Leicester for delivery elsewhere. Thus, as in 1898, over a third of the traffic was local. Tolls brought in only £875, other sources contributing £1,642. The upkeep of the navigation cost almost exactly the same as it had earned in tolls – £874. In view of this modest outlay on the works, it is hardly surprising that the verdict on their condition was only 'Fair'.

The Leicester Navigation and amalgamations

Changes of ownership by amalgamation or takeover were by no means unknown in the Leicester Navigation's area. During the hectic days of the railway mania, the Midland Railway Company had got its hands on the Ashby and Oakham Canals, the result being that the latter went out of existence, while the Grantham Canal, which was in some respects a competitor of the Melton Navigation, passed into railway control in 1854. But the Leicester line itself remained untouched. The first hint of possible reorganization to meet the challenge of the railways came as early as 1845, when the Leicester, Loughborough, and Erewash got together to discuss amalgamation. Unfortunately, as so often, the three companies could not agree, and this commonsense union failed to materialize, the delegates contenting themselves with a kind of treaty pledging their companies not to part with any line or section of their systems if this would prejudice the interests of the other companies, or break the through line of waterways. Unfortunately, this was made conditional on the rest of the companies of the line doing the same, and both the Grand Junction and the Leicestershire & Northamptonshire Union refused to have anything to do with it. As Sir Francis Head, the Grand Junction chairman, explained, it was not that his company had anything against it, but they had no intention of disposing of any part of their system – if they had, their Act would have prevented any such 'perversion', and anyway the proposed pledge would need the approval of a General Assembly. The Loughborough thereupon said that they regarded the pledge as at an end, and they were considering disposing of their undertaking altogether. This naturally caused much alarm among the other companies of the line, but nothing came of it. The Leicester, on the other hand, found the communication of the Grand Junction reassuring, and said that they still held themselves bound by the pledge.[16]

Having failed to get an amalgamation, the Leicester tried to get at least a certain amount of unity among the Leicester line companies by advocating that they, together with the Loughborough and Erewash, should lease the Leicestershire & Northamptonshire Union for not more than twenty-one years. The Leicestershire & Northamptonshire Union agreed, asking £8,581 10s. a year (which amounted to £4 10s [£4.50] per share). As the Leicestershire & Northamptonshire Union's dividend at this time was rather higher than this, the price was not unreasonable, and in February 1846 all four companies appointed delegates to negotiate the lease. However, the project came to nothing – perhaps fortunately for the three northern companies, in view of the decline of trade on the Leicestershire & Northamptonshire Union in the period during which it might have been leased to them.

The Leicester's views on leasing or selling their undertaking were later modified in view of their decreasing trade, and in 1863 they were one of the companies sending delegates to a meeting of canal companies to discuss amalgamation. Whether the committee were sufficiently well disposed towards any of their neighbours to contemplate amalgamating with them is doubtful. The Loughborough and Erewash were always exasperating, the Leicestershire & Northamptonshire Union and Grand Union were in an even worse financial position than the Leicester, while an acrimonious dispute broke out with the Grand Junction in 1865 over the sinking of the Grand Junction's steamboat *Gnat* on the Leicester Navigation. The Grand Junction blamed the poor state of the waterway, while the Leicester had some bitter things to say about the steerer of the steamboat. They seem to have had a good argument on their side, but paid compensation to the Grand Junction for the sake of harmony – a gesture completely ruined by their action in slapping an extra 1d. per ton on merchandise to Leicester, presumably to compensate for possible further destruction by Grand Junction boats; that at least is what the Grand Junction must have thought, and they protested heatedly.

The first definite approach to the Leicester about taking the concern over came in 1887, when a London syndicate came to them with a scheme for developing internal waterways, and asked the Leicester to name a price for the sale of their line. The committee adopted the same attitude as the southern companies of the Leicester line approached by the syndicate, professing themselves quite willing to sell, but refusing to give a price until a full-scale valuation had been made. As they made it clear that this would have to be paid for by the syndicate, and as it would have been expensive and not necessarily followed by any direct result, the matter naturally lapsed at this point.[17]

Several years elapsed before another approach was made. This time it came from the Grand Junction, whose efforts to develop trade on the Leicester line in the 1890s have been noted. On 16 October 1894, Hubert Thomas, the Grand Junction clerk, wrote to the Leicester after going through their accounts, commenting on their 'fast declining revenue'. Having bought the Grand Union and Leicestershire & Northamptonshire Union, and so owning the entire waterway from London to Leicester outright, the Grand Junction were now prepared to take the matter further and either buy the Leicester outright, or negotiate an agreement on through-tolls with them. He asked them to name their price, and, to encourage a realistic assessment, pointed out their heavy annual commitments in millers' compensation payments and towpath rents, in all, some £130. The Leicester's chairman, John Bennett, Dawes, and the clerk having been asked to study the subject, the undertaking was offered to the Grand Junction at the price of £70 per £140 share. This was refused, and a through-toll agreement negotiated instead. It was to run for seven years from 1 October 1895, and, if the works at Foxton and Watford on the former Grand Union had been completed by then, was to be extended for fifteen years from 1 January 1897. This would bring it into line with agreements with the Loughborough and Erewash the Grand Junction had concluded. The Grand Junction were to have the option of buying the Leicester with all its assets at £70 per share. The Grand Junction guaranteed the Leicester tolls of £300 a year on through traffic, but if the option to purchase were not exercised by 1 January 1900, the guarantee was to be raised to £350 until the end of the agreement. If the Grand Junction did buy the Leicester, they would pay for the Act, and a fixed sum towards associated costs.[18]

In connection with this agreement there is an illuminating passage in a letter from Dr F.W. Bennett to Hubert Thomas (3 December 1896) which shows a rather casual attitude on the part of the Leicester's governing body. Bennett says 'The fact is, however, that nobody is sufficiently interested in Canal matters to make it worth while to put any steam into them. If we had our living to get by them, we should act with more energy and also pay closer attention to what seem trifles. I am certain your Company would soon put a different face on matters'. The implication is that the committee ran the navigation company as much as a pastime as a business concern, just as a manufacturer might have a farm to amuse his leisure hours, and this attitude would certainly help to explain the supine direction of the Leicester and of their neighbours the Union Canals in their later years. It cost little to buy a holding in the Leicester; the £141 shares fetched only £33 during the 1890s and there was a slight return in the form of dividends. The committee was an amateur body, dividing fees of £40 annually among them for attendance at meetings, and the clerk and senior officers were part-time, and not the important people their equivalents on the railways were – the manager, for instance, visited the works on the navigation on his bicycle. All in all there was little inducement to reorganize or modernize the navigation. By this date the committee was similar in composition to those of the neighbouring Leicestershire & Northamptonshire Union and Grand Union, local interests having taken over completely. It is true that there was a hard core of expert knowledge – men like Dawes on the

Leicester and Foxton on the Leicestershire & Northamptonshire Union, who had considerable experience of the Leicester line either as traders on it or as former officers of one or other of the companies, or even, as in the case of both Foxton and Dawes, as both. But so far as can be ascertained, most committee members were interested in running their canals (attendance records at committee meetings were quite good) but had no special knowledge of the niceties of inland waterway management. Of those who were on the committee in the company's later years, Dr F.W. Bennett, for instance, was a distinguished ear specialist and an authority on Leicestershire geology, J.H. Taylor was a brewer by trade and an authority on antiques, and J.D. Cradock was for many years secretary of the Quorn Hunt and the oldest hunt follower in the Midlands.

The Grand Junction at first found the prospect of taking over the Leicester satisfactory, and the 1894 agreement was duly extended in 1897, the Grand Junction subcommittee moreover recommending that the Leicester, Loughborough and Erewash be bought. But a more cautious note soon appeared, and on the approach of the agreement's expiry date for the option to purchase the Leicester (1 January 1900), the Grand Junction asked the Leicester for an extension of time.[19] Thomas explained that the building of the Foxton inclined plane had been held up by 'strikes and other circumstances', and until this was finished they could not go ahead with the Watford locks' alterations (another part of their scheme to improve the line to Leicester), and so could not judge how trade would react. The Leicester committee refused even to discuss it, however; the Grand Junction must, they said, exercise their option to purchase by 1 January 1900 or not at all. As often happened, the three northern canals were again out of step, for the Loughborough and Erewash had already agreed to an extension. The Grand Junction subcommittee therefore flatly refused to recommend buying the Leicester.[20] The Loughborough purchase, too, was given up, and, although representatives of the three companies met to discuss what action to take with the Grand Junction, the matter dropped for a time.[21] It was not until 1903, with tonnages declining exceptionally steeply, that the Leicester took the matter up again, jointly with the Loughborough and Erewash. The three offered their undertakings to the Grand Junction, the Leicester's price being £21,900, which did not include certain properties, among them, curiously, the Navigation Inn at Barrow and the Honeypot osier-bed at Cossington.[22] The Grand Junction, however, in view of the complete absence of the revival of trade on the Leicester line they had expected, refused all three.

By 1911, the Grand Junction's disenchantment with their effort to revive the Leicester line was complete; failure was all too evident – though the Leicester's tonnages had picked up after a bad start, falling from £796 in 1900 to £704 in 1903, but rising to £1,070 in 1910. On 29 March 1911, the committee considered a letter from John W. Bliss, the Grand Junction's clerk, in which it was pointed out that the Grand Junction had paid the Leicester £844 under the guarantee clauses of the agreement, and that they were not disposed to continue such a loss. In fact, if the Leicester did not agree to waive the guarantee, they would refuse to renew the through-toll agreement when it became terminable on 1 January 1912. The Leicester declined to do this, and asserted that, as tolls had been lowered from 4d. to 2½d. per ton, the Grand Junction's loss was nothing like the figure they gave.[23] The Grand Junction were persuaded not to terminate the agreement, partly by the traders on the line led by Fellows, Morton and Clayton, partly by the improved tonnage figures – since if the increase of traffic were maintained, no payment under the guarantee would be necessary.[24]

The question of the guarantee came up again in 1916, when the Grand Junction asked for a reduction in the amount guaranteed, as they had been compelled to pay £150 to the Leicester under it. The Leicester granted a reduction from £350 to £250 but would not make it retrospective. Having considered the matter further, the Grand Junction gave notice that they intended to end the through-toll agreement on 31 December 1916. But this did not please the canal traders, and Fellows, Morton and Clayton, who had been instrumental in saving the through-toll pact before, now appealed again to the Leicester, asking that the rate should be continued at the same figure as on 31 December 1916; the committee, however, refused unless the Grand Junction restored their guarantee. Evidently Fellows, Morton and Clayton had been withholding their tolls in the hope that the old rate might be restored, but the committee peremptorily ordered that they should pay up at once and, rejecting the carriers' suggestion of arbitration, threatened legal action. Matters were resolved in 1918 by the Canal Control Commission, who asked the Leicester to continue through-tolls at the old rate without charging the Grand Junction, as the government would in any event make up the net revenue. Tolls remained in this state until 1921, when, in collaboration with the Ministry of Transport, a 150 per cent increase was introduced.[25] This did not indicate an increasing prosperity; in 1924, shares were still being quoted at £32.

The first intimation of events which were to bring the independent existence of the Leicester Navigation to a close, came in 1930. It took the form of an approach by the Grand Union Canal Company, which was formed by the amalgamation of a number of independent companies in 1929, and should not to be confused with the Grand Union which formed part of the Leicester line from its opening in 1814. The new Grand Union, anxious to increase trade on the waterways by large-scale operations, considered taking over not only the Leicester, but also the Loughborough and Erewash as well.[26] The Leicester was not unwilling, and agreed to appoint a valuer. The negotiations went quite happily. The question of the Reserve Fund, which had been a difficulty in earlier takeover bids, was settled amicably, and, although an unexpected hitch did occur when the Grand Union rejected the figure of £4,682 which the accountants of both companies had agreed for certain wharves, water rights, etc., and insisted on £2,600–700 instead, this too was settled. On 2 January 1931, the Leicester's Chairman, W.W. Harding, was able to report to the General Meeting that he and Curtis, the Grand Union's chairman, had provisionally agreed that the Grand Union should pay £26,282 for the Leicester plus £1,900 compensation for officers and others, and a sum equal to the market value of the securities of the Reserve Fund (at this date £17,116) fifteen days before the date of completion of the sale. The agreement was approved unanimously by a Special General Meeting on 21 April 1931; as a commentary on the interest of the shareholders in their navigation, it may be mentioned that the meeting was attended by twelve people, mostly committee members.[27] Leonard Bygrave, the Grand Union secretary, came on to the committee of the Leicester to represent Grand Union interests.

The Grand Union Canal (Leicester Canals Purchase etc.) Act 1931 (21 & 22 Geo V, c 107) received the Royal Assent on 31 July 1931. The price the Grand Union were to pay for the Leicester Navigation was now fixed at £26,032, and was not to include certain property in Belgrave Gate which was to be sold to its occupiers, Messrs Cotton and Austin, or the money the Leicester had invested in mortgage or in other stocks or cash at the bank, or unclaimed dividends. The Reserve Fund was also excluded, but was to be taken by the Grand Union at middle market price. The Grand Union were to pay the costs of the Act, including vendor's costs, and also compensation for loss of office to the Leicester's chairman (£200), the committee (£800 to be divided between the members), clerk (J.T. Salusbury, £500), manager (J.L. Baxter, £250), accountant (L. Freeman, £100) and a clerk (H.A. England, £50). The vesting date, on which the purchase money was to be paid, was

Bridge, dated 1960 in the brickwork, which carried the mineral line over the Leicester Navigation. The granite wharf is visible in the background

1 January following the passing of the Act, from which date the Leicester was to be merged with the Grand Union. In the event, the Grand Union took over the contract for the sale of the Belgrave Gate land, and this, included in the purchase money paid to the Leicester, brought the grand total up to £48,126 10s. (£48,126.50), of which £17,496 was the price of the Leicester's investments.[28]

It remained only for the committee to tidy up a few loose ends, among them the distribution of the £800 compensation allowed to them. They disposed of £20 of it in a gracious gesture, by giving it as a gratuity to Kirk, the company's lockwright for many years. Each of the committee members received £25 from the remainder, and what was left was divided among them according to the frequency of their attendance at committee meetings. Only five were present at their last meeting, on 10 December 1931, though vacancies on the committee had not been filled in recent years. It must seem fitting, to those with a sense of continuity of history, that one of those at this last meeting was H.A. Dawes, a name which had been closely connected with the Leicester for many years.

CHAPTER 6
The Leicester Navigation Today

With its incorporation in the Grand Union, the Leicester ceased to have an independent life of its own, and therefore much significance outside the broad strategy of the great concern which had swallowed it. The activities of the Grand Union demand treatment in a volume of their own; here all that can be done is to point out that they were no more successful in reviving trade on the Leicester line than the Grand Junction had been, and to indicate the trend of events on the former Leicester Navigation in recent times.

In *The Leicester line*, the evidence of L.T.C. Rolt's *Narrow Boat* and Susan Woolfitt's *Idle Women* was cited to show the state of the southern canals of the Leicester line in the last years before nationalization. It is interesting to see what these highly perceptive observers saw in the Leicester. Mr Rolt found the line through Leicester unattractive and polluted, with a hint of danger in the side channels and weirs of the flood works. He was lucky enough to travel along the stretch north of Cossington, where the navigation can alone be called attractive, in high summer when it looks at its lush best; but he makes no mention of traffic, presumably because he met none. With unerring judgement, he picked out the Navigation Inn at Barrow, once the property of the Leicester Navigation Company and now one of the few unspoiled canal pubs in the county. Mrs Woolfitt's boats were piloted down the river by a waterman; it was the practice, she says, to offer this service to all the boats, as the waterway was a river navigation.[2] On the return journey, despite a light lading and the pilot, the boats went aground several times, for the whole line badly needed dredging.[3] Again, there is no reference to traffic on the Leicester, though several pairs of boats were passed on the Erewash, most of which would presumably have been heading for the Leicester line.

Near Birstall on the Leicester Navigation

Under the Transport Act of 1947, the Grand Union system became part of the nationalized British Transport Waterways. A survey of traffic over the waterways in 1954 showed that in the previous four years, tonnage on the Grand Union had decreased by 14 per cent, but most of this was caused at London and Birmingham. Receipts on the Leicester line between Leicester and the Trent had in fact fallen steeply from £17,137 in 1951 to £12,233 in 1953. To offset this, expenditure had fallen from £23,715 in 1951 to £19,250 in 1953, but there was still a deficit of £6,578 in the former year, £7,017 in the latter. Tolls were a mere £809 in 1951 and £663 in 1953 – in each case, this amounted to only about 10 per cent of the revenue from wharfage and warehousing, and was less even than the water rents. Nevertheless, the Leicester, as part of the line between Leicester and the Trent, was one of the few waterways singled out by the North Midland Regional Board for Industry, which recommended that this line should be improved, a process involving considerable capital expenditure, so that barges loaded in the Humber could travel direct to Leicester without trans-shipment of cargo at Nottingham. Leicester, the board thought, offered scope for additional waterborne traffic if better facilities were offered. The Board of Survey which undertook this report did not accept this, for the line was not included in their Group I waterways – those recommended for development – but they did include the whole of the Grand Union above Berkhamsted in Group II – waterways to be retained.[4]

The British Waterways Board, set up by the Transport Act in 1962, took over supervision of the nationalized system on 1 January 1963, and by the end of that year had produced an interim report.[5] Their view of the prospects of the Leicester line as a whole were slightly more pessimistic than their predecessors. Commercially, they pointed out that goods came from the Humber by boat to Nottingham – but were then brought to Leicester by road. There was not much pleasure-traffic, and the board felt that the question of whether they would be justified in maintaining the Leicester line to pleasure-traffic standards needed careful thought. They did suggest that the line from the Trent to Leicester should be retained in the proposed pleasure-traffic network, but south of Leicester was ranked only with 'other possibilities' and

Cossington lock on the Leicester Navigation, 1955

without this the Leicester would have lost a great deal of its significance as a pleasure-cruising waterway. For general recreation and amenity – walking, angling, etc. – the whole Leicester line from the Trent to the Grand Junction was rightly commended.

This judicious report was followed in 1965 by a summary of the position and a general survey of British waterways for the benefit of the growing number of people to whom their future was becoming a matter of great concern.[6] In this, the section from Leicester to the Trent, comprising the former Leicester and Loughborough Navigations, is dealt with as a unity. There seems to have been a change of mind about its use by pleasure-craft since 1963, for the navigation is now said to be 'popular with pleasure-craft both for cruising and mooring', though this is qualified as referring especially to the Loughborough Navigation section. The gross receipts for 1964 were £4,985, of which £2,430 came from pleasure craft and £1,002 from water sales. Maintenance work cost £13,984, an average of £559 per mile. The total deficit was £15,268. Both income and expenditure were less than in 1963, when the former had been £4,547 (of which £2,764 came from boats) and the latter £25,017, giving a deficit of £20,470. The board had little hope of making any saving on this line, for even if they converted it to an unnavigable water channel, this would only have reduced the deficit to about £13,500 a year.

Luckily, the navigation had an ever-increasing number of friends – not only among those who lived in the area and had boats on it, but boatowners and hire firms from far afield. While it has to be admitted that the former Leicester Navigation is dull in its Leicester reaches, rather repellent in the Thurmaston–Wanlip area (where gravel workings cause the surrounding land to have the appearance of a First World War battlefield, and the distinctive odours of the sewage farm have to be sampled to be believed), and charming only from Cossington onwards, and then only in parts, it has one vitally important feature: it is an essential link between the deadwater canals of the north and the south. Without it, or any of the rest of the Leicester line, the possibilities of lengthy canal cruises would be far more limited. In addition, several firms building and hiring boats have opened depots on the line, and a body of well-informed support is provided by the Soar Valley Cruising Association. Moreover, Leicester at last woke up to the fact that it had a potential amenity. A plan to develop a riverside walk along the Leicester Navigation from its heart to Belgrave put forward in 1956 was shelved, but in 1972, led by the Leicester Civic Society, a survey of the waterway through Leicester was undertaken. The towpath was said to be in parts like an assault course, and the old adage about having 'everything but the kitchen sink' in the waterway was falsified when one of these objects was actually fished out of a lock.[7] Later even more peculiar items emerged, including a box of ammunition from the Second World War. A plan for the development of the riverside land was drawn up. Whether this will be such as to please the hardened boater, who often prefers the savage squalor of the waterways of Birmingham and Stoke-on-Trent to the tame insipidities of a public park, is doubtful, but in any event, most of the relics of interest to the industrial archaeologist which had survived the flood works of the nineteenth century have been swept away in post-war fits of over-enthusiastic planning, including, for instance, remains of the L & SR.

But even if, from the enthusiast's point of view (and after all, he is not the one who has to live there) these developments turn out to be misguided, it does show that people are beginning to care about 'this useful work' the Leicester Navigation, though it no longer supplies Leicester, as it should, with 'coal, limestone, and granite of its neighbourhood' and with 'timber, deals, and various articles of home consumption'.[8]

CHAPTER 7

The Melton Mowbray Navigation

The celebrated dictum that 'happy is the country that has no history' was certainly true of the Melton Mowbray Navigation. It is only in the early days of its formation, when it shared the Leicester's struggles with the Leicestershire coalowners, and towards the end of its life, when it was being mortally wounded by railways, that it emerges from obscurity. In the interim, what little evidence there is seems to show the company as having an uneventful, prosperous career. Most regrettably, the records of the Melton Company are lost; they may have disappeared when the firm which acted as clerks to the company for the whole of its life moved their premises in 1907.[1] The history of the navigation can therefore only be seen through the eyes of others.

From the first, the Melton Navigation was closely connected with the Leicester, and indeed at times during the development of the two projects they were, for practical purposes, one. As early as 13 February 1779, the Leicester Navigation promoters, in outlining their scheme, included a branch to Melton Mowbray as part of it. Melton patriotism was aroused by this Leicester encroachment, and a letter in the *Leicester Journal* on 3 June 1780 vigorously repudiated the suggestion that this line to Melton should be a part of the Leicester Navigation – though the latter was welcome as a 'cousin' to the Melton. It seems that this 'hands off Melton' attitude had some effect, for Jessop's 1785 survey, it was implied at the time, did not include a Melton branch. Later in 1785 however, Melton was evidently incorporated, for by 28 September there was talk of carrying the line on to Oakham.

Matters became more explicit at the meeting in Leicester Castle on 20 October 1785. Here a petition in favour of a Bill for the Leicester Navigation was postponed to the following month, so that plans and estimates for a navigation along the River Wreake to Melton could be produced.[2] On 29 October 1785, the *Leicester Journal* reported that Jessop was at work on this survey, and that £6,000 had been subscribed towards this 'Reke Navigation' on the first day the subscription list was opened.[3] By 5 November, the amount subscribed was such as to encourage Lord Harborough (a strong supporter of the Melton project), the Hon. Gerrard Noel Edwards, and other influential Rutland landowners to ask Jessop to look at the River Eye (in effect, the River Wreake above Melton Mowbray) to see whether it could be used to continue the navigation towards Oakham. Jessop's reply must have been unfavourable, but the Melton scheme went on, the first recorded meeting of promoters being held at the Swan Inn, Melton Mowbray, on 12 November 1785. The bankers taking subscriptions for it were Mansfield (Leicester) and Stokes (Melton Mowbray). All this activity meant that a full report could be made to the postponed Leicester Navigation meeting on 24 November, which was sufficiently impressed to include among its resolutions one favouring the extension of navigation to Melton, and to Oakham if practicable.[4] Figures were produced in the press to show that coal consumed at Melton amounted to 12,000 tons a year – 4,000 from Coleorton and 8,000 from Derbyshire. If a navigation were available, Leicestershire coal would sell in Melton at 7d. or 7½d. per cwt, half the existing price. The Melton promoters, thus encouraged, summoned a meeting on 22 December 1785, but postponed it until 19 January 1786, when they learned that the Leicester Navigation had produced another plan 'of still more general utility' than theirs. This rather left a related scheme, for a canal from Melton by way of Oakham to Stamford, out on a limb, as its promoters had fixed their meeting for 24 December. They went ahead nevertheless, setting up a committee to arrange a survey.[5]

Whatever changes the Leicester Navigation promoters suggested were adopted by the Melton party, and a new form of petition to incorporate them was drawn up by order of a meeting on 21 January 1786, at which a number of influential men, led by the Earls of Harborough and Winchilsea, were present, and which unanimously resolved to apply for leave to petition for a Bill.[6]

The revised petition was studied at a meeting on 6 February 1786. It was ordered that 5 per cent of the subscriptions should be paid on or before 21 February 1786, and Joseph Noble of Melton Mowbray was appointed treasurer to collect them – though Mansfield (Leicester) and Abel Smith (Nottingham) were also authorized to receive subscription money. The meeting then considered the petition, and took an important decision. The project depended on the Leicester Navigation, since physically the Melton was an offshoot from it; if that scheme failed to get through Parliament, the Melton automatically failed with it. It was known that there was powerful opposition among the west Leicestershire coalowners to the Leicester scheme. Therefore, as an insurance against the failure of the Leicester, the Melton promoters decided to petition for a navigation from Melton to Loughborough, the extension from Cossington to Loughborough being along the Soar.[7] In a way, this did the Leicester a disservice; opponents said that the Melton promoters had taken this step because they realized that the Forest line was impossible.[8]

William Pochin, one of the county MPs, presented the Melton's petition on 1 March 1786, the same day as the other county MP, John Peach Hungerford, presented the Leicester's.[9] On 13 May 1786, the Leicester's Bill failed at its second reading. In theory, the Melton could still have gone ahead, but the promoter's courage failed them, and after some hesitation they withdrew their Bill, and a meeting was held at the Ram Inn, Melton Mowbray, on 3 June 1786 to clear up debts.[10] The meeting was not wholly a success; as late as May 1788, the normally placable Jessop began proceedings to get his bill for a survey paid, and the promoters had to exhort their subscribers to attend a special meeting as a matter of urgency.[11]

As in the case of the Leicester Navigation project, this setback seems to have inhibited further effort for some time, but by 1789 the promoters' spirits had revived sufficiently for them to put a notice in the *Journal* advertising a renewal of the application for an Act to sanction the construction of a navigation from Melton Mowbray to Loughborough.[12] A meeting at the Black Swan, Melton, on 9 February 1789 resolved to raise a subscription for this purpose, those who took part in the first application being asked to signify whether they wanted to subscribe to this one too. The solicitors appointed to record the subscribers were James Parke and Charles Latham, whose firm was to hold the clerkship of the Melton Navigation for the whole of its history. So encouraging was the response that the promoters, with those engaged on reviving the Leicester Navigation scheme, summoned a meeting at the Exchange, Leicester, the chair being taken by Joseph Cradock, a public-spirited landowner well known for his support of navigation schemes in the county. Nearly £14,000 was subscribed at this meeting.[13] It seems that the two schemes had once more come together as a single project for a navigation from Loughborough to Leicester and Melton Mowbray, but

AN

ACT

FOR

Making Navigable the Rivers *Wreak* and *Eye*, from the Junction of the ſaid River *Wreak* with the intended Navigation from *Loughborough* to *Leiceſter*, at or near a certain Place called *Turnwater Meadow*, in the Lordſhip of *Coſſington*, to *Mill Cloſe Homeſtead*, in the Pariſh of *Melton Mowbray*, all in the County of *Leiceſter*.

WHEREAS a Communication by Water between the River *Trent* and the Town of *Melton Mowbray*, in the County of *Leiceſter*, would be productive of great public Advantage, as well as particular local Benefit to the ſaid Town, and the Neighbourhood thereof, by rendering the Carriage of Coal, Stone, Lime, Lime Stone, Timber, Lead, and all Kinds of Merchandize, to the ſaid Town and Neighbourhood, and to ſeveral Parts of the Counties of *Leiceſter*, *Lincoln*, and *Rutland*, much cheaper and eaſier than it is at preſent: — Preamble.

And whereas Application is making to Parliament for an Act form a Navigable Communication from the *Loughborough* Canal 'igation (which falls into the River *Trent*) to the Junction of River *Soar* with the River *Wreak*, and from thence up 'd River *Wreak* to *Turnwater Meadow*, in the Lordſhip of 'on, and from thence to *Leiceſter*:

A And

First page of the Act of 1791 for the Melton Mowbray Navigation local men were still kept in office – Joseph Noble, for instance, remained as treasurer for subscribers in the Melton area. There is, in fact, a definite reference to 'the intended Navigation-bill from Loughborough to Leicester and Melton-Mowbray' in the agenda of a meeting on 11 March 1789, and a call on the entire undertaking of 2 per cent was made, Latham being the receiver at Melton.[14] Over the next few months, however, the two projects again drifted apart. On 16 July 1790, a meeting chaired by Lord Rawdon approved the motion of applying once more for an Act to authorize the Loughborough–Leicester and Forest lines, and added that if the plan to make the Wreake navigable to Melton were brought forward again, they would support it.[15] They went further, and sent one of their leading promoters, Dr Robert Bree, to offer support at a meeting at the White Swan, Melton, on 27 July – a meeting which was attended by local landowners like Lord Harborough, and, more unexpectedly, by Lord Ferrers, whose mineral interests in west Leicestershire had for long put him in the ranks of the opponents of the Leicester. The meeting passed resolutions in favour of canalizing the Wreake from the Leicester Navigation to Mill Close Homestead in Melton Mowbray.[16] The notice of the promoters' intention of applying for Parliamentary powers to effect this appeared in the *Journal* on 10 September 1790. Joseph Noble remained the treasurer, and in the months ahead a 2 per cent call was made, and a further one on 29 April 1791. It is interesting to note that, in addition to the local banks at Melton, Leicester and Nottingham, subscriptions could be paid into the London bank of Samuel Smith, Son, and Co.[17] The Bill went through all its stages rapidly, and received the Royal Assent on 5 July 1791 (31 Geo III, c 76).

The company's first Act

The natural starting point for the Melton Line was the junction of the Soar and the Wreake at Cossington. However, the deviation forced on the Leicester Navigation to avoid Wanlip led the Act to stipulate a starting point about a mile upstream along the Wreake, at a remote spot known as Turnwater Meadow, midway between the villages of Cossington and Syston. The line terminated in the Mill Close Homestead in Melton Mowbray, alongside the Oakham road, where its former existence is commemorated today by the Boat Inn which stood near it. The total length was 14 miles 4 furlongs 5 chains, and the rise from the junction to Melton was 70 ft 11 in. This was achieved by twelve

Junction of the Leicester and Melton Mowbray Navigation at Turnwater Meadow

locks, which were built broad. Three of these – Ratcliffe Meadow, Washstones, and Kirby Bellars – were constructed to overcome natural difficulties (the first at the confluence of a tributary stream, the other two in connection with the removal of awkward bends), and the rest were on cuts made to avoid water mills. The Melton was cursed with a plethora of these, no fewer than nine: Syston, Ratcliffe, Rearsby, Thrussington, Brooksby, Hoby, Frisby, Asfordby, and Eye Kettleby. The meandering nature of the Wreake, from which it may have derived its Scandinavian name, has been pointed out, and some twenty cuts were made to remove the worst of the bends. Most of the cuts were quite small, the most extensive being the one made in Melton Mowbray across the Play Close, which the company had to make to avoid the ground of William Reeve. The cuts at Eye Kettleby and Kirby Bellars were also quite extensive, and the former gave the navigation its deepest lock, the rise being 8 ft 7 in.

The work of making all this navigable was to be done on behalf of eighty-six named individuals duly incorporated as 'The Company of Proprietors of the Navigation from the Leicester Navigation to Melton

Mowbray in the County of Leicester'. This cumbersome title was the only official one the company ever had; they normally called themselves, on official notices, the Melton Mowbray Navigation, or more briefly the Melton Canal. The title 'Wreake & Eye Navigation', sometimes applied to this undertaking, was seldom or never used by the company themselves. The usual vested interests were protected, one case being rather ominous for the future. This was a mill in Melton Mowbray parish quaintly known as Two Eye mill, driven by the waters of the Scalford Brook, a feeder of the Eye: the protective clause explained its concern with the mill by saying that the waters of the Eye are very low in summer – an unpromising statement for the prospects of a navigation company, and one which proved in later years to be only too true. The company had to tread a delicate path in dealing with Church and State, for, while the mill was the property of the bishop of Ely, another stretch of its line in Melton, through the Play Close and Causey Hill Close, was hedged in by protective clauses in favour of Viscount Melbourne. William Reeve, not content with obtaining a cut deviating the line round his mansion house, secured further protection from annoyance by a clause forbidding the company to erect any building or wharf by this cut. Outside Melton Mowbray, however, there were few restrictions on the making of the navigation; deviation from the planned line was of course restricted, the width of cuts and towpaths was limited, and rent was to be paid to the landowners for the latter. The usual enormous number of commissioners to settle disputes appeared, with an elaborate series of regulations to govern the handling of these. It took the Act forty-nine clauses to get these preliminaries out of the way, and the important matter of finance appears with clause 50, which authorized the proprietors to raise 250 shares, of not more than £100 value each. Each shareholder was to have a vote at meetings for every share he held to a maximum of ten. If the maximum total of £25,000 proved insufficient, the proprietors could raise a further £5,000 among themselves, or by admitting new subscribers, or by mortgaging the tolls. During the making of the navigation, proprietors were to be paid interest at the rate of 5 per cent.

There were to be two General Assemblies of the proprietors every year, the first to be held at the White Swan, Melton Mowbray, on the first Wednesday after the Act came into force. After this, they were to be held on the first Wednesday in January and July each year at 11 a.m., the place being fixed by the previous General Assembly. At the first General Assembly, the proprietors were required to elect a committee of not more than thirteen, nor fewer than nine, and a clerk or clerks and such officers as they thought necessary. All officers handling money in the course of their duties were to give security. The clerk was to be the chief executive officer, attending all Assemblies and committee meetings and seeing that the instructions of these bodies were carried out. The committee were to report to the General Assembly, and at each July meeting an election of the committee was to be held. They were to meet monthly until the navigation was completed, and then as often as necessary. Each committee member had one vote at meetings, and the chairman a casting vote.

If a minimum of ten proprietors thought that a Special Assembly should consider any topic, they could order one to be summoned. The purpose of such a meeting was to be advertised in the Leicester newspaper. Neither a Special nor a General Assembly could elect a committee unless fifty shares were represented at the meeting, either in person or by proxy. If a meeting failed by reason of such representation not being present, another meeting was to be summoned for two months later, and proprietors not being present at this second meeting in person or by proxy were to have 5s. (25p) stopped out of their next dividend.

General Assemblies were empowered to make calls on the proprietors to finance the construction of the works, but these were limited to £10 per call, and there was to be an interval of at least two calendar months between calls. They could also make by-laws regulating the use of the navigation.

The maximum tonnage rates permitted by the Act were:

Coal from the Leicester Navigation to Eye Kettleby, Sysonby or Melton – 2s. 6d. (25p) per ton.

Coal as above not passing as far as Eye Kettleby, etc. – 2½d. per ton-mile.

Iron, timber, and other goods, wares and merchandise (except as below) from the Leicester Navigation to Eye Kettleby, Sysonby or Melton – 4s. (20p) per ton.

Iron, etc., as above not passing so far as Eye Kettleby, etc. – 4d. per ton-mile.

Lime, limestone, stones for building, materials for paving and repairing roads – half the coal rate.

A fraction of a mile was to count as one mile, fractions of tons by quarters.

Some materials were exempt from toll: dung, marl, coal ashes, turf, and all other manure (not lime) for lands in parishes adjoining the line,

Millers not to draw down the Water lower than a certain Height.

Provided always, That no Occupier or Miller of any Mill or Mills on the Line of the ſaid intended Navigation ſhall at any Time after the Commencement of this Act draw down, or ſuffer to be drawn down, the Water which at preſent ſupplies ſuch Mill or Mills, lower than Six Inches below the Heighth of a full Pond, and alſo that the Occupier or Miller of every ſuch Mill ſhall keep the Flood Gates in ſuch good and ſubſtantial Repair as at all Times to prevent any conſiderable Quantity of Water from leaking through the ſame; and in caſe any ſuch Miller or Occupier ſhall draw down the Water lower than Six Inches below the Heighth of a full Pond, or ſhall neglect or refuſe to keep the Flood Gates belonging to his Mill or Mills in ſuch Repair as aforeſaid, every Perſon offending in either of the Ways aforeſaid ſhall for every ſuch Offence forfeit and pay the Sum of Forty Shillings to the ſaid Company of Proprietors; and in caſe of Neglect or Refuſal of Payment of ſuch Forfeiture, on Demand, then and in ſuch Caſe it ſhall be recovered and levied in ſuch Manner as is hereinbefore directed in Caſes of other Forfeitures incurred under this Act; and in caſe any Occupier of a Mill belonging to the ſaid Company of Proprietors ſhall be convicted as aforeſaid, then and in ſuch Caſe ſuch Forfeiture ſhall be paid to the Perſon informing againſt ſuch Occupier for ſuch Offence.

Extract from the 1791 Act, Melton Mowbray Navigation

and also materials for making and repairing any public or private road. But to qualify for exemption, these were not to pass through a lock while the water was not running over the 'Gauge Paddle or Waste Weir'. Also exempt from toll were pleasure boats used by owners of lands adjoining the navigation, but these were not to pass through a lock.

The rates were the maximum the company could levy. The actual tonnages, which could be any figure below this tariff, were to be fixed by the first General Assembly, and they could be lowered by a subsequent General Assembly's giving three months notice, and raised by any later Assembly.

Masters of boats were to give accounts of their lading, and the commissioners were to determine whether any difference between what the master said the weight should be and what it really was could be attributed to absorption of moisture since it was originally gauged. The only exception was to be lime coming from the Leicester Navigation in boxes with the Leicester's mark showing the height; these were to be accepted at this figure.

As a river navigation, the Melton had special problems, and some of these were dealt with by separate clauses. If a ford were injured by the navigation – i.e. made so deep that it became difficult or impossible to ford it – the company were to make amends by providing alternative means of crossing; ferries are mentioned, though a bridge would presumably have been the normal substitute. Millers were to carry out the company's instructions regarding drawing off water during construction. They were not at any time to draw off water lower than 6 in below a full pond. If their mills were damaged by the navigation, they could require the company to buy them within twelve months of the completion of the undertaking. Disputes between the millers and the company were to be resolved by the commissioners. The company's servants were given special powers to enter lands to carry out emergency flood works – a wise precaution with the Wreake.

Control was to be exercised over the masters of boats on the navigation. Masters were required to have their names painted in white letters at least 6 in high on each side of their boats, and the company were to put marks on the outsides to show the depth of a boat in the water at various ladings. They were not to obstruct the navigation by mooring across it, nor were they to moor by any mill, dam or bridge, or near Reeve's house in Melton Mowbray. On the other hand, the company were required to make suitable places where boats could turn or pass one another. As the use of wide boats from the Trent was envisaged, this could be an important point on a smallish river like the Wreake. Distance posts were to be put up near each lock, and the first boat to reach one of them had the right of way through the lock, the others then taking turns. Masters of boats going uphill had to empty the locks after they had passed through them. Penalties were attached to all these clauses, and there was a general one against wasting water, the fine ranging from £1 to £5. An offender caught emptying ballast into the navigation, however, did not have the possibility of a light fine to look forward to – for this a flat £5 was laid down.

Finally, the Melton was required to take a share in the compensation payment the Leicester had been forced to offer the Loughborough as the price for the withdrawal of the latter's opposition to the Leicester's Bill. The present Act laid down that if in any year compensation became payable to the Loughborough, the Melton were to pay one sixth of this by way of reimbursement to the Leicester.[18]

13. That no boatman shall let down the cloughs of the upper or lower gates of any lock, without making use of a winch, and turning them so as to let them go down *gently*, under the penalty of *forty shillings*.

14. That no boatman driving a horse, or going forward to fill locks, shall go over any person's ground instead of the towing-path, under the penalty of *twenty shillings*.

15. That no person shall un-moor a boat lying for its turn, and put his own in its place, under the penalty of *forty shillings*.

16. That all boatmen bringing loaded boats to the public wharf, shall deliver their lading as soon as possible, and not let their boats remain longer than is necessary when another boat is waiting for its turn, under the penalty of *forty shillings*.

17. That all boatmen with vessels placed in the Navigation so as to obstruct the passage, shall immediately remove on request, under the penalty of *five shillings*, and an additional *five shillings* for every hour his boat shall continue to obstruct the passage.

18. That every person shall have the plate number of his vessel legible, so as not to prevent the guaging of it, under the penalty of *five pounds*.

19. That no master or owner of any vessel, shall alter the number of any such vessel, without immediate notice being given to the Collector of Tolls, under the penalty of *five pounds*.

Page from the book of Rules and Bye-laws of the Melton Mowbray Navigation, 1844

Construction

Plans and specifications for the construction of the navigation were soon ready, and were available for would-be contractors to inspect at the White Swan on the day of the first General Assembly (6 July 1791), and afterwards at the offices of the clerks, Parke and Latham, in Melton Mowbray. The committee met to award the contracts at the Ram Inn, Melton Mowbray, on 31 August. Unfortunately, in the absence of the company's records, it is impossible to say to whom or at what price the contracts went, other than that W. Shaw at Frisby in 1793 and Robert Hollingshead at Melton in the same year were engaging labour (navvies, brickmakers, bricklayers and carpenters) for work on the navigation, and were probably the contractors for these sections. The whole work was under the general supervision of Christopher Staveley junior, who, in view of the work he was doing on the Leicester Navigation and the Leicestershire & Northamptonshire Union at this time, must have been a very busy man. Despite this, in June 1793, he managed to find time to marry Miss Ella of Loughborough, doubtless a member of the family which was to be foremost among the traders on the Leicester Navigation in its early years. The frequency of the calls indicates a fair rate of progress: 5 per cent had been called by the time the Act was passed, and after this 5 per cent calls were made until by 24 May 1793, £45 had been called on each £100 share. After this, either because major works were being undertaken or because of rising costs, calls were normally of 10 per cent and at the legal minimum of two months apart. The full £100 was reached with a 5 per cent call on 9 May 1794. The works were, however, still by no means finished. The General Assembly on 2 July 1794 was told that a further £3,750 would be required. They decided to raise this by further calls on the shares, to the extent of £15 per share.[19] The first call on this extra capital was of £10 and was made at once, and the remaining £5 was called for by 1 November. Nevertheless, the amount produced was insufficient, and a further call of £5 was made on the day of the January 1795 General Assembly, and was no doubt approved by that meeting. By March, however, it was clear that money was still needed; and the company was having difficulty in getting some of its subscribers to pay up, with threats of forfeiture being sent out to defaulters – a sorry come-down from the days when Melton shares were so eagerly sought after that they commanded a premium of £18 4s. (£18.20) or more.[20] A special General Assembly was summoned to consider ways of raising the £2,500 Staveley said was needed to finish the works. The Assembly met at the White Swan on 30 March 1795, and sanctioned raising this sum. According to the *Leicester Herald*, this was to be done by a £10 per share call.[21] This was not advertised, however; it may have been put into action by circularizing the proprietors individually, or possibly as a loan from them rather than a call on their shares, for in 1804 it was reported that the company were about to pay off 'the Whole of the Money advanced by the Proprietors', although the company's efforts to solve their financial problems piecemeal make certainty impossible.[22]

Little is known of the progress of the works – the only recorded trouble was the pilfering of tools and equipment endemic to constructional sites at all times. One of the culprits was caught, but was too poor to be worth prosecuting. His offence was stealing some deal boards in 1795 'after the late floods', which perhaps gives a hint of more serious troubles.[23] The enrolments of conveyances of lands to the company give some information, though the company were somewhat erratic, enrolling some transactions with the clerk of the peace and not others, behaviour which was to be criticized by Parliament later. Land for the basin in Melton was bought from the Earl of Harborough, who had himself procured it only recently, perhaps for this purpose. It comprised some 5 acres, lying to the east side of the turnpike road from Melton to Oakham, and the company paid £525 for it. In 1800, they sold the 3 acres they had not used.

The hazards attached to buying the considerable amount of land required, in relatively small lots from numerous owners, are illustrated by the curious case of Thrussington mill. Under the clause of the Act concerning the purchase of mills affected by the navigation, the company are required to buy Thrussington mill, with sundry pieces of land totalling about 2 acres, from the apparent owner, William Dracott of Asfordby. This they did, by indenture of 25 May 1792, at the price of £240. Unfortunately for the company, no sooner had they taken possession of the mill than Joseph Dracott, of Kings Langley, Herts, turned up, claiming to be the rightful owner, a claim which he succeeded in establishing to the company's satisfaction. Even so, there was apparently a third possible claimant who was not in the country, and whose whereabouts were unknown. The company managed to arrange a compromise by which they paid Joseph £190, but he undertook to repay it if a better claim subsequently appeared. None seems to have done, and the company held Thrussington mill until 1801, when they sold it for £250.

Bridge and lock at Hoby on the Melton Navigation

The company seem to have been made to pay through the nose for some of the land they bought. Land around Melton Mowbray was then fetching about £100 an acre, but the company had to pay much higher prices; for example a small parcel of 2 roods 9 perches, needed to make a cut at Hoby mill cost £41 3s. 3d. (£41.16). Most of the land they wanted was in the form of small pieces required for cuts to avoid mills or to eliminate bends in the very winding Wreake.

Progress of construction cannot be followed in detail. It would seem that work was carried on at several points simultaneously. The contracts for the locks at Thrussington mill and Kirby Bellars were, for instance, let at the same time.[24] The half-yearly meeting of the Leicester Navigation held on 6 January 1794 was told that 'in a few days' boats would be able to pass up the Melton as far as Rearsby.[25] By the end of October 1794, the navigation was open to Frisby mill.[26] The date of the opening to Melton Mowbray is unknown. No coal had arrived there by water by 2 January 1795, so presumably the navigation was still not open, although the *Leicester Herald* confidently announced that coal traffic to Melton would commence on 7 January.[27] But in March 1795 'the passage of boats' over the whole line was still not possible.[28] The company did not set about appointing a toll collector in Melton Mowbray until mid-1795, the committee being authorized to engage one at their meeting on 25 June.[29] Navigation probably commenced soon after this; at any rate, a Melton agent was trying to hire a boat for use on the navigation in late November.[30]

It is possible that the company's constructional activities were slowed down in the later stages of the work by lack of money. As has been seen, they had to raise £2,500 above the amount they had already overdrawn. They were soon in trouble elsewhere, too. Owners of lands adjoining the navigation blamed them for damage by the floods of 1795, and held a meeting at Hoby to discuss getting legal redress. This was smoothed over, but trouble with the landowners in this respect continued to harass the company for many years, protest meetings of the former becoming a regular feature. On the other hand, an active body which did not clash with the company but if anything helped them, or rather their users, existed in the Wreake and Eye Humane Society. Its purpose was to minimize the danger to human life from the river: as for instance in 1800, when a reward was paid by the society to a number of men who rescued a boatman employed by William Sutton, a leading trader on the Melton, when he fell into the river near the junction.[31]

The company soon came to the same conclusion as the Leicester Navigation in similar circumstances: they had been too modest in fixing their toll maximum – though they can be excused for not anticipating the great rise in prices in the 1790s which had caused their line to be more costly to make than expected. This, coupled with chronic indebtedness, led them after experimenting with toll increases in 1798, to consider getting an Act to allow them to clear their debts and raise tolls to a higher figure than was permitted by the 1791 Act. This they did in 1800, by an Act (40 Geo III, c 55) which gained the Royal Assent on 20 June 1800. The preamble stated that the company had nearly completed the works, but in the process had spent all their £25,000 authorized and £5,000 reserve capital, plus all the tolls (about £7,000), and were £4,000 in debt. The Act authorized them to raise a further £10,000, which would make the cost of the completed navigation about £43,000. They were also granted the power to take the following additional tonnage rates over and above those already authorized. Coal from the Leicester Navigation to Eye Kettleby, Sysonby or Melton Mowbray, but not travelling as far as the fifth lock on the Oakham Canal (near Brentingby) was to pay 1s. (5p) per ton; if it went to the fifth lock, it would pay 6d.

Mile-post formerly near Ratcliffe-on-the-Wreake (now in Leicester Museum)

($2\frac{1}{2}$) per ton; if not so far as Eye Kettleby, 1d. per ton per mile. Other goods (apart from lime, limestone, and stone for building or road making, which paid half the coal rate) were to be charged 1s. 6d. ($7\frac{1}{2}$p) per ton if passing beyond Eye Kettleby but not so far as the fifth lock on the Oakham, or if they passed from the Oakham or Melton Mowbray to the Leicester; if they were carried more than 5 miles on the Melton and thence to the fifth lock on the Oakham, 9d. per ton; if carried on the Melton but not to Eye Kettleby, or from the Oakham but not so far as the Leicester $1\frac{1}{2}$d. per ton per mile. Goods passing from the Oakham on to the Melton, but no further than the basin at Melton Mowbray, were exempt from these additional tolls, as were materials being taken for the construction of the Oakham Canal. The Act cast a disapproving eye on the Melton's land conveyancing methods, and ordered them to enroll all conveyances in future (they were legally bound to do so already, but obviously had been remiss).

The period of prosperity

Because of the drawback or rebate paid by the Leicester company to the Melton for coal, accounts were kept of the quantities of coal passing on to the Melton from the Leicester, and whether the individual cargoes were for the Melton Navigation or the Oakham Canal. Fortunately, a few of the earliest accounts have survived, and the following table summarizes the amounts involved:

Half year ending	Coal tonnage to the Melton tons	Coal tonnage to the Oakham tons
June 1800	5,199½	1,154
December 1800	5,714¾	540
June 1801	4,121¾	1,379
December 1801	4,476	676
June 1802	3,560	649

At the busiest, this did not mean more than between thirty and forty boats a month, and the average was fewer than this. The seasonal variations in trade due to the Melton's being a river navigation and therefore liable to be shallower in summer than winter emerges clearly from the returns, for while the average tonnage carried in the winter months was 37–9 tons, and 40 tons was quite common, in midsummer boats were travelling with 25 tons or even less. Of course, there would have been boats which, carrying cargoes not qualifying for a drawback, were not recorded, but there is no doubt that coal was the chief trade on the Melton; probably the only other commodity of much importance was lime, in great demand as a fertilizer.

It will be noted that there is a decline after December 1800. The series is too short, however, to indicate whether this was due to the extra tonnage imposed by the company under its new Act, if indeed they did impose them. They were certainly thinking of raising tolls in 1801, but their decision is not recorded.[32] The question of putting the tonnages up to the full authorized rate had been discussed in 1799, and this may have contributed to the fall in traffic. Increasing the tolls does not seem to have been the right answer, for in 1803 it was proposed to reduce them, at least on general merchandise and in the following year a group of the Melton's proprietors formed a company to sell coal at the wharf in Melton, the agent being William Rowell, of the Toll House.[33]

Whether these activities were a cause or an effect of an upward turn in the company's affairs cannot be known, but certainly things seem to have improved from that point. In 1802, a merchant in Melton was offering to supply Swedish or Russian iron, cooper's staves, hemp, flax, bristles, or other imported merchandise to order, and a cabinet-maker and timber dealer had already built sheds and drying houses for seasoning timber by the Public Wharf. The value of the waterway to the country through which it ran was recognized: when Rotherby Hall was put up for letting, the notice called attention to the fact that the house was 'supplied with fine Pit Coal at an easy rate' from the nearby navigation.

One of the causes of the development of the Melton into a flourishing concern must have been the coming of the Oakham Canal, which, commencing at the Melton's basin in Melton Mowbray, continued the line of navigable waterway by an artificial cut to Oakham, from where an extensive land sale was developed to Uppingham and Stamford. The Oakham, authorized in 1793, was opened in stages, the line to Oakham being probably completed in 1803. The researches of Mr D.H. Tew have shown that as early as 1806, from a total of nearly 19,000 tons of goods of all kinds passing on to the Melton, at least 10,935 continued on to the Oakham, while in 1812, the quantity travelling beyond Melton was

The Old Basin, Burton Street, Melton Mowbray

12,308 out of 21,710 tons. By the 1840s, the Melton were very dependent on the Oakham Canal, only one-third of their trade not passing on to it.

The development of the Melton Navigation into a prosperous concern is shown by the increasing dividends. In 1804, the company, in announcing its intention of paying off all the loans from its proprietors, also said that they would pay a dividend of £2 8s. (£2.40) per share on the original capital.[34] In 1807, it was noted that the company paid £8 per share in the previous year, and were likely to pay more in future.[35] In 1818, the dividend was £8 10s. (£8.50).[36] Shares in the Melton stood at £255 in 1824, which obviously indicates that good dividends were being paid. In 1845, the last full year of the Melton's undisputed supremacy as a transport system in east Leicestershire, it paid £13 per share. For a brief period, these high dividends continued; only £8 was paid in 1846, it is true, but the 1847 dividend was no less than £14. After this, as will be seen, dividends slumped spectacularly.[37]

With a built-in growth rate of this order, the Melton had little cause for complaint; but they naturally got involved in the wranglings over tolls endemic to the Leicester line, since they depended on the three northern companies of that line. Normally the Melton were on reasonably good terms with the Leicester; the two companies shared the cost of the 1790 survey between them, the Melton paying one-third, while at a later date Swinburne, the Leicester's toll collector in Loughborough, was ordered to let the Melton have (at a price) copies of his books containing information relating to the boats he gauged.[38] When the Leicester refused a reduction in tolls on boats from Loughborough to Leicester, they granted one on those passing on to the Melton.[39] The Melton were naturally concerned by the Leicester's proposal to get Parliamentary powers to raise their rates, but were pacified by the Leicester's offering to take an extra 3d. per ton on coal passing on to the Melton, of which 1d. would be granted to the Melton.[40] Payments were made under this agreement, though they were not large – in the early days, up to £28 per half year, but often much less.

The Leicester were taken by surprise when, in 1799, the Melton announced their intention to petition for an Act to raise their tolls, and when Caldecott, the Melton's chairman, rejected their proposals for modifications, they appealed to the local MPs. They seem to have taken no further action and as they had done the same thing themselves in 1797, they had no real right to complain. Good relations were restored, for they appointed Ferneley from the Melton to the Loughborough toll collectorship in 1804, and in 1806 called on Neale, the

Melton's agent, to arbitrate in one of their perennial disputes with the millers on their line.

A letter to the Leicester Navigation Company in 1818 pointed out the existence of a rival, the Grantham Canal. The carrying firm of Ella, Coleman and Co. wrote to say that most goods for Melton on the Grantham Canal went along that line to Hickling Wharf, some 9 miles from Melton, paying 1s. 7$\frac{1}{2}$d. (8$\frac{1}{2}$p) per ton. By the Melton Navigation route, the tonnage was 7s. 3d. (36p). Ella, Coleman and Co. suggested cuts by the Loughborough, Leicester, and Melton Navigations to reduce this to 4s. 3d. (21p), when they would lower their carriage charges by 2s. (10p). The Leicester agreed, providing the Loughborough and Melton did so too. In view of the Melton's handsome dividends, it seems unlikely that they were losing very much trade.[41]

In 1841, the most serious dispute recorded between the Melton and the Leicester occurred. The Leicester had reduced coal tolls, but not enough in the Melton's opinion. They demanded a further lowering of the tolls on coal coming on to the Melton, so that the Leicester should not take more than 4d. per ton. The Leicester, in reply, fired a warning shot by publicly announcing their intention of raising their coal tolls to the legal maximum, the idea being to upset not only the Melton, but also the line's traders; the committee recorded that there was no need to act on the notice at present, obviously expecting that the threat would be sufficient. It was. On 12 January 1842 the Melton climbed down, and agreed to reduce tolls on coal passing on to the Melton but not the Oakham by one-third. The Leicester thereupon granted the 4d. per ton rate on coal on to the Melton, and harmony was restored.[42]

Decline and fall

The time when the companies of the Leicester line could afford the luxury of quarrelling with one another was drawing to an end. By 1842, it was clear that railway competition was established and dangerous; and the Melton decided to take steps to put their house in order. To forestall any assertion that the company exploited their near-monopoly of bulk transport in the area, a meeting was summoned to consider reducing coal tolls, and a statement of the amount of coal carried over the preceding three years was sent to each proprietor. It is worth looking at these returns in some detail, since they give one of the few surviving glimpses of this successful waterway pretty near to the pinnacle of its prosperity.

The totals for the three years were:

	tons
1839	10,974½
1840	11,777½
1841	9,657

The drop shown in 1841 was spread over most of the wharves on the navigation, the biggest being in Melton, where 7,156½ tons in 1840 fell to 5,459½ tons in 1841. Curiously enough, the wharves nearest the Midland Counties Railway line, where trade might have been expected to disappear, showed an increase. However, in the case of Lewin bridge, this only meant one extra boat, while Syston had visits from two boats instead of one.

The coal was landed at eleven wharves on the navigation. Some of these were little more than spots where the odd cargo of coal could be dropped for local sale – such as Hoby and Kirby Bellars, neither of which received any consignments in 1839. Hoby got 21½ tons in 1840 and 24½

Kirby Bellars: bed of the Melton Navigation

tons in 1841, and Kirby Bellars 42 tons in the former and 40 tons in the latter year. The most important wharf was naturally Melton, with 6,244 tons, 7,156½ tons, and 5,459½ tons in the three years covered, and next came Rearsby wharf, with 2,888½ tons, 2,868 tons, and 2,595½ tons. None of the other wharves handled anything like these quantities. In order of importance, they were Thrussington (618, 669, and 573 tons); Lewin bridge, where the Fosse Way crossed the Navigation (553, 448, and 484 tons); Brooksby (279, 269, and 234 tons), Asfordby (198, 125, and 83 tons); Ratcliffe (72, 94, and 56 tons); Frisby (50, 41½, and 27½ tons); and Syston (72, 42, and 79½ tons).

The figures for coal traffic to Melton by road are also given for the period 1 October 1841 to 1 January 1842; 598 tons, against 2,813½ tons taken along the navigation in the same period.[43]

By 1844, the threat of railway invasion had become evident. The Midland Counties Railway had been steadily eating into the Leicester Navigation's traffic since 1840. In 1844 it merged with two neighbouring companies to form the Midland Railway – a great concern with an ambitious and energetic chairman, George Hudson, whose watchword was 'expansion'. Among the first projects the new railway company put forward was one for a line from its main Derby–Leicester line at Syston to Peterborough, to tap the resources of East Anglia. The projected line ran through the heart of the territory served by the Melton Navigation, and indeed followed it closely along the Wreake valley to Melton, whence it followed approximately the course of the Oakham Canal to Oakham. It is unnecessary to discuss here the conflicts (including physical ones) surrounding the making of this line, which form one of the most fascinating chapters of British railway history.[44] The fact which was so important to the Melton Navigation was that one of the actions the Midland proposed to take to buy off the furious opposition was to purchase the Oakham Canal with the idea of closing it and using part of its line as a route for the railway.

The companies of the Leicester line held a meeting in Loughborough on 15 November 1844 to discuss this and the proposed Erewash Valley railway, the Melton being represented by their chairman, Marriott, the Revd Mr Stephens, and a Mr Fabling who is likely to have been the steward of the Earl of Harborough, the great landowner who was to literally fight the railway's attempts to encroach on Stapleford Park in the following years. The meeting agreed to oppose both projects, but when it came to putting a case to the Parliamentary Committee taking evidence, they put up a poor show. It may be wondered whether they really understood how serious the threat was. Most of the witnesses do not seem to have considered that, should the Oakham be closed, not only would the Melton lose its through trade, but its local traffic would be threatened as well. For example James Sutton, a carrier, thought that whatever happened to the Oakham, the Melton would keep a share of their trade, while George Hornbuckle Betts, an Oakham Canal committee member, was even more optimistic, believing that the Melton's trade to Melton Mowbray would be untouched. William Latham, the Melton's clerk, seems to have shared this view, but pointed out that two-thirds of the Melton's traffic went on to the Oakham, and that if this trade were lost, 'our canal would be worth scarcely anything; it would not pay the expenses of keeping it open'. Although he was thus anticipating that his company might lose two-thirds of their trade, it does not seem to have struck him that the other third might vanish as well. He agreed that if coal could be transferred from boat to rail at Melton, it would get to Oakham more cheaply, but there were no facilities for such interchange, or indeed any connection between the navigation and the proposed railway. He admitted that the threat of the railway had brought down the Melton's tolls from the $2\frac{3}{4}$d. of 'six or seven years ago' to $1\frac{3}{4}$d. per ton introduced about six months before, and now to 1d. per ton, with $\frac{1}{2}$d. extra for haulage. The railway's permitted maximum toll on coal was $1\frac{1}{4}$d. per ton, and the Melton intended to charge this, but were prepared to knock a further $\frac{1}{4}$d. off if they found this was necessary to keep their traffic. 'As long as we can get any dividend we shall carry.' These were brave words, but in concluding, Latham dropped a hint that if the Oakham were purchased, the Melton should be bought too. The Midland Railway was naturally not interested.[45]

Opposition was in vain: the Midland Railway Company got Acts authorizing the construction of the Syston and Peterborough Railway, and the purchase and closure of the Oakham Canal was sanctioned in 1846. Melton Mowbray was now the terminus of navigation, and the result, as reflected in the company's dividends, was dramatic. In 1847, the Melton was still able to pay £14 per share, but in 1848 no dividend was declared, as was the case in 1849 and 1850 also. Dividends were paid after this, as shown overleaf.[46]

The Leicester treated the Melton sympathetically in view of their 'great diminution, amounting almost to a total loss' of trade, and tolls were lowered to preserve what was left. The toll on coal for the Melton, for instance, was lowered to 1d. per ton on 18 October 1849, and that on

Dividends per share

	£	s.	d.			£	s.	d.	
1851		15	0	(75p)	1861		15	0	(75p)
1852		–			1862		–		
1853		–			1863		14	0	(70p)
1854	1	0	0		1864		11	0	(55p)
1855	1	1	11	(£1.09½)	1865		–		
1856	1	2	0	(£1.10)	1866		8	0	(40p)
1857		–			1867		10	0	(50p)
1858		–			1868		–		
1859	1	0	0		1869		5	0	(25p)
1860		–							

lime from 3½d. to 2½d. per ton the next month.[47] There was some success with the coal trade, which rose to 3,069 tons in the next three months (the previous three months had seen only 1,369 tons pass up the Melton), but the Loughborough and Erewash, never very considerate of the well-being of other companies, put up their tolls at the end of the year, and the Leicester felt constrained to do the same. It was more than two years before they were forced to reduce the rate from 3d. to 2d., and by that time the railway had devoured the trade.[48] Tolls then went down to 1d. at Latham's request in 1853, and this may have encouraged an increase of trade, reflected in the slightly better dividends for the ensuing years.[49]

There was little the impoverished company could do with their concern other than sell it, and both the Loughborough Navigation and the Midland Railway refused to buy. Their income hardly allowed the works to be kept up to first class standards, and witnesses before committees hearing evidence relating to a projected railway in east Leicestershire could in 1872 refer to it as dilapidated. Though a certain amount of coal was still being sold from Rearsby wharf, there was very little traffic, and the navigation was 'in such bad repair that it will soon have to be closed'.[50]

It is therefore evident that by the 1870s the possibility of closure was being contemplated, but matters dragged on until 1876 before moves were made to bring this about. Then, perhaps because of concern over the safety of bridges carrying public roads over the navigation, the company began to think of bringing their affairs to a close. As their shares at this time stood at £2 to £3, it was unlikely that there would be any opposition from the proprietors, who were therefore summoned to a Special General Meeting at the Harborough Hotel, Melton Mowbray, on 5 July 1876, with 'Mr Monk of Nottingham' in the chair. On examining the accounts, it was seen that there had been more deterioration of the works in the preceding year than in the previous four years. E.H. Clarke thereupon proposed, Fitton seconded, and it was carried unanimously that the necessary steps should be taken for getting Parliamentary powers to close the undertaking. This was amended to give the committee the necessary powers to press on with this.[51] A further meeting was held at the Harborough Hotel on 5 February 1877 with G. Fitton in the chair, when final confirmation was given to the decision.[52] The Melton Highway Board, arguing that the impoverished company would agree to rebuild its bridges to suit them rather than face opposition in Parliament, set up a subcommittee to negotiate this.[53] The two sides met, and the company accepted the Highway Board's offer to take over responsibility for the bridges for a payment of £100.[54] Arrangements for the closure went ahead, despite which an advertisement for the sale of Brooksby Hall mentioned as an asset that the estate had a wharf on the navigation!

There was a certain amount of opposition to the closure from some of the landowners on the grounds that they got 'large quantities' of coal, lime, and manure from Leicester and other places by way of the Melton. Their real objection, however, seems to have been their fear of what would happen if nobody was responsible for sluices and weirs, since the Bill in its original form said nothing about what was to happen about water levels. They were also concerned that no safeguards were written into the Bill to see that the company made a good job of the work they were required to do in dismantling the locks, etc. Other points to which they objected were that the company sought to dispose of buildings and other works as they thought fit, was not bound to give owners of adjacent lands a right of pre-emption, and would extinguish rights of way. However, the company proved amenable, making amendments in the Bill, and the landowners' petition was at the last moment withdrawn. The Act (Melton Mowbray Navigation (Abandonment) Act, 1877; 40 & 41 Vic, c 78) received the Royal Assent on 12 July 1877. It authorized a closing of the navigation from 1 August 1877. The company was to compensate landowners in respect of any works they had hitherto had to maintain and which would now fall upon the latter, and were to restore bridges, after which their liability for these was to cease.

Kirby Bellars lock on the Melton Navigation

Channels to existing locks were to be left open, and the upper gates at each were to be replaced by a weir and the lower gates removed. Arrangements were made to settle disputes. From 1 August 1877, the company existed solely to wind up its own affairs.

The company's public notice of closure was dated 31 July, the day before the closing date, but did not appear in the *Leicester Journal* until 10 August, requiring all boats to be removed from the waterway by the 14th. This may have been the origin of the local story that one boat did not know that the navigation was closing down and got shut in permanently in the basin at Melton Mowbray! A meeting of the landowners was held at the George, Melton, on 4 September, to discuss compensation and arrangements with the millowners for lowering the weirs.[55] The Local Board had already begun considering the flood gates at Sysonby lock, which they visited and had their surveyor report on, together with the fate of the basin, about which they corresponded with the company's engineer, Macaulay. By March 1878, the bridge here was being demolished, and the road to Oakham widened.[56] On 29 May 1878, the Local Board saw a plan submitted by the company to develop the site of the basin for housing, but the board would not agree to this. They were not on particularly good terms with the company at the time, on account of disagreement between the two as to which bridges were the company's responsibility and which the board's. One rather surprising feature is that the company admitted liability for the road from Asfordby railway station to the Leicester road, and agreed to repair it before handing over.

The basin continued to give trouble, and complaints of a bad smell from it were received by the board on 24 July 1878, but nothing was done about it.[57] But later in 1878, the basin was bought by the Midland Railway Company. In 1881, it was reported that the Midland was laying down a siding for the purpose of filling in the canal basin 'and when the Company gets fully at work in that direction the canal will very soon be a thing of the past'.[58]

'A thing of the past' the navigation may have been, but these few complacent words commemorate a concern which had served the east Leicestershire community well. Even today, when much of the former charm of Melton Mowbray has been sacrificed in the interests of

Bridge near Frisby-on-Wreake on the Melton Mowbray Navigation

supermarkets and motor cars, the town's inhabitants have pleasant reminders of their canal: its line across the Play Close, marked by a handsome avenue of trees, and a riverside footpath to Eye Kettleby, the former canal towpath, preserved as a right of way by immemorial usage, which the Local Board nobly fought for, for future Meltonians, in 1878.[59]

And further down the navigation, despite brutal defilement of the landscape around Asfordby and Frisby, there is much to delight the lover of the quiet Leicestershire landscape: lush meadows and the greenest grass in England, with only the ruins of an occasional lock or a dried-up cut through a village cricket field to tell that once upon a time it was a busy water highway.

APPENDIX 1

Income, Expenditure, and Dividends of the Leicester Navigation

Year	Income £	Expenditure £	Dividend £140 shares £
1791			
1792			
1793			
1794			
1795			
1796			
1797			
1798			7
1799			4
1800	10,298	5,388	2
1801	11,406	7,223	8
1802	9,854	5,958	7
1803	11,540	7,028	7
1804	10,884	6,615	7
1805	10,650	6,923	7
1806	11,097	6,944	7½
1807	9,993	6,245	6
1808	12,619	7,072	9
1809	10,579	7,281	5

Year	Income £	Expenditure £	Dividend £140 shares £
1810	10,369	5,058	9½
1811	12,908	8,555	9
1812	7,886	2,812	8½
1813	9,126	2,741	10
1814	9,155	3,095	10
1815	10,356	6,945	12
1816	8,965	5,811	11½
1817	9,293	1,598	10½
1818	10,205	2,720	12½
1819	10,470	3,354	14
1820	11,287	3,866	12
1821	11,566	4,035	13
1822	11,342	4,061	13
1823	12,540	3,766	14
1824	12,524	4,038	16
1825	19,027	10,233	16
1826	13,162	3,598	16
1827	12,788	3,954	17
1828	13,610	4,142	16
1829	12,498	3,014	18
1830	12,888	3,140	16
1831	12,876	3,339	16½
1832	12,266	4,837	16
1833	11,184	5,916	11
1834	9,021	5,491	10
1835	8,361	2,787	10
1836	10,993	2,569	12
1837	11,245	2,602	15½
1838	11,189	3,279	14
1839	10,867	2,670	14
1840	9,010	2,356	14
1841	7,645	1,836	11
1842	6,871	2,289	10
1843	7,207	2,375	9
1844	7,466	2,422	8½
1845	8,547	3,074	8½

Year	Income £	Expenditure £	Dividend £140 shares £
1846	8,341	3,237	8
1847	8,977	2,506	9
1848	6,379	3,278	8
1849	6,086	2,405	$5\frac{1}{2}$
1850	6,201	2,104	6
1851	5,013	2,056	$5\frac{1}{2}$
1852	4,701	1,921	5
1853	4,586	1,780	$4\frac{1}{4}$
1854	3,907	1,748	4
1855	3,956	1,683	$3\frac{1}{4}$
1856	3,669	1,625	3
1857	3,463	1,617	3
1858	3,193	1,718	$2\frac{5}{8}$
1859	3,305	1,457	$2\frac{3}{4}$
1860	3,485	1,705	$2\frac{3}{4}$
1861	3,275	1,570	$2\frac{5}{8}$
1862	3,333	1,431	$2\frac{3}{4}$
1863	3,465	1,635	$3\frac{1}{4}$
1864	3,512	1,663	$3\frac{1}{4}$
1865	3,360	1,348	3
1866	3,406	1,401	3
1867	3,230	1,406	$2\frac{3}{4}$
1868	3,428	1,477	3
1869	3,369	1,318	$2\frac{7}{8}$
1870	3,341	1,351	3
1871	2,953	1,272	$2\frac{3}{4}$
1872	2,964	1,237	$2\frac{5}{8}$
1873	3,011	1,319	$2\frac{5}{8}$
1874	2,884	1,555	$2\frac{3}{4}$
1875	2,751	1,344	$2\frac{5}{8}$
1876	2,718	1,269	$2\frac{5}{8}$
1877	2,612	1,263	$2\frac{5}{8}$
1878	2,473	1,081	$2\frac{1}{2}$
1879	2,345	1,181	$2\frac{1}{2}$
1880	2,426	1,203	$2\frac{7}{8}$
1881	2,363	1,175	$2\frac{3}{4}$

Year	Income £	Expenditure £	Dividend £140 shares £
1882	2,477	1,179	$2\frac{5}{8}$
1883	2,190	1,087	$2\frac{1}{4}$
1884	2,403	1,121	$2\frac{1}{4}$
1885	2,189	1,064	$2\frac{3}{8}$
1886	2,292	1,076	2
1887	2,356	1,166	$2\frac{1}{4}$
1888	2,392	1,140	$2\frac{1}{4}$
1889	2,305	1,136	$2\frac{1}{4}$
1890	2,316	1,088	$2\frac{1}{8}$
1891	2,216	976	$2\frac{1}{4}$
1892	2,281	1,000	$2\frac{1}{4}$
1893	2,183	986	$2\frac{1}{2}$
1894	2,274	1,029	$2\frac{1}{8}$
1895	2,418	985	$2\frac{1}{4}$
1896	2,147	983	$2\frac{3}{8}$
1897	2,224	1,072	$2\frac{1}{8}$
1898	2,323	1,053	$2\frac{3}{10}$
1899	2,205	1,071	$2\frac{7}{40}$
1900	2,038	1,065	$2\frac{7}{40}$
1901	2,077	1,121	$2\frac{7}{8}$
1902	2,101	1,098	$2\frac{1}{20}$
1903	2,386	1,100	$2\frac{1}{4}$
1904	2,369	1,139	$2\frac{1}{8}$
1905	2,517	1,160	$2\frac{3}{20}$
1906	2,495	1,088	$2\frac{3}{10}$
1907	2,455	1,124	$2\frac{3}{10}$
1908	2,487	1,114	$2\frac{1}{5}$
1909	2,630	1,138	$2\frac{9}{20}$
1910	2,654	1,134	$2\frac{1}{2}$
1911	2,864	1,215	$2\frac{27}{40}$
1912	2,764	1,148	$2\frac{23}{40}$
1913	2,865	1,284	$2\frac{7}{10}$
1914	3,103	1,390	$2\frac{3}{4}$
1915	2,970	1,415	$2\frac{7}{8}$
1916	2,769	1,373	$2\frac{1}{4}$
1917	2,845	1,438	$1\frac{9}{10}$

Year	Income £	Expenditure £	Dividend £140 shares £
1918	2,733	1,021	$1\frac{39}{40}$
1919	3,523	1,231	$1\frac{3}{4}$
1920	5,066	2,135	2
1921	4,232	2,641	$3\frac{1}{20}$
1922	4,450	2,443	$3\frac{1}{4}$
1923	3,531	2,370	$2\frac{31}{40}$
1924	3,461	2,092	$2\frac{1}{8}$
1925	3,937	2,042	$3\frac{5}{8}$
1926	3,537	2,072	$3\frac{5}{8}$
1927	3,722	2,132	$3\frac{1}{8}$
1928	3,888	2,376	$3\frac{5}{8}$
1929	3,712	2,387	3
1930	3,444	2,014	$3\frac{1}{6}$
1931	1,624	992	3

APPENDIX 2

Locks on the Leicester Navigation

Lock	Length		Breadth		Depth on sill		Fall	
	ft	in	ft	in	ft	in	ft	in
North	84	6	15	0	4	2	4	7
Lime-kiln	88	6	15	6	4	5	4	3
Belgrave	88	6	15	6	4	4	3	11
Birstall	86	0	15	0	4	6	3	4
Thurmaston	85	6	15	0	4	2	3	2
Junction	86	0	15	0	4	3	4	9
Cossington	85	0	15	0	4	4	5	3
Sileby	85	0	15	0	4	2	4	6
Mountsorrel	86	0	15	0	3	11	4	1
Barrow-on-Soar	86	0	15	0	3	10	9	7
Flood (Pilling's)	86	0	15	0	4	0	–	

(The above dimensions are those given in the 1898 Traffic Returns.)

APPENDIX 3

Locks on the Melton Mowbray Navigation

Lock		Distance from previous lock			Rise	
		m	f	ch	ft	in
Syston mill	From junction	0	3	9	7	1
Ratcliffe meadow		1	1	6	3	3
Ratcliffe mill		0	6	0	5	7
Rearsby mill		1	0	4	5	6
Thrussington mill		1	3	3	6	4
Brooksby mill		1	0	6	7	4
Hoby mill		1	1	2	5	4
Washstones ford		1	2	8	5	9
Frisby mill		0	6	5	5	1
Asfordby mill		1	0	3	6	1
Kirby Bellars		1	4	7	5	0
Eye Kettleby mill		1	1	6	8	7
To Mill Close homestead		1	3	6		
Total length of navigation		14	4	5		

(The above distances are those given by Staveley in his 1790 survey, and were confirmed as accurate at the closure of the navigation in 1877.)

APPENDIX 4

Melton Mowbray Navigation Accounts, year ending 1 July 1806

	£	s.	d.	£	s.	d.
Receipts						
Tolls on 'upgate' (eastbound) traffic						
Coal and coke (17,744 tons)						
Lime (568 tons)						
Timber and deals (135½ tons)						
Stone (39½ tons)						
Slates (37 tons)						
Bricks (23½ tons)						
Merchandise (428¾ tons)	2,498	5	10			
Tolls on 'back' (westbound) traffic						
Grain (328 tons)						
Wool (217¼ tons)						
Timber (126¼ tons)						
Merchandise (38 tons)	150	9	1½			
Year's drawback from Leicester Navigation	30	7	6½			
Sundries	32	10	2	4,973	13	6

	£	s.	d.	£	s.	d.
Expenditure						
Salaries:						
Clerk	30	0	0			
Agent	63	0	0			
Toll Collector at the Junction	52	10	0			
'Extra salary for last year'	5	3	10½			
Toll Collector at Melton	21	0	0	171	13	10½
New Work				20	9	0
Cleaning the Navigation				25	8	9
Rents of Towing Paths				19	6	1
Repairs of Navigation				17	2	9
'To Millers stopping Mills'				8	6	6
Paid off old debts				192	16	5
Expenses of General and Committee meetings				31	15	6
Levies				10	1	10½
Property Tax				94	7	6
Stationery				16	7	4
'Dridging Boat'				156	7	0
Sundries				3	3	0
		Balance		1,806	7	11
				4,973	13	6

(From information supplied by Mr D.H. Tew.)

Notes

As extensive use has been made of the minutes of the Leicester Navigation Company, references to them have only been quoted to cover important points. Where no reference is given for a statement in the text, it will normally have been based on these minutes.

Chapter 1

1 *Leicester Journal*, 21 June, 15 November 1777.
2 *LJ*, 18 September 1779, 22 April 1780.
3 *LJ*, 7 November 1778.
4 *LJ*, 17 November 1787.
5 *LJ*, 30 January 1779.
6 *LJ*, 13 March 1779.
7 *LJ*, 13 February 1779.
8 *LJ*, 20 May 1780. It was the practice to pay for shares in a new venture like this in instalments known as calls.
9 *LJ*, 27 May 1780.
10 *LJ*, 17 June 1780.
11 *LJ*, 27 May 1780.
12 *LJ*, 3 June 1780.
13 *LJ*, 3 September 1785.
14 *LJ*, 21 May 1785.
15 *LJ*, 28 May 1785.
16 *LJ*, 4 June 1785.
17 *LJ*, 25 June 1785.
18 *LJ*, 16 July 1785, quoting *Cambridge Journal* 9 July 1785.
19 *LJ*, 3 September 1785.
20 *LJ*, 17 September 1785.
21 *LJ*, 10 September 1785.
22 *LJ*, 24 September 1785. The editorial cited Ralph Allen's tramroad at the Bath stone quarries as a successful example.
23 *LJ*, 1 October 1785.

24 *LJ*, 22 October 1785.
25 *LJ*, 22 October 1785.
26 *LJ*, 29 October 1785.
27 *LJ*, 29 October 1785.
28 *LJ*, 19 November 1785.
29 *LJ*, 5 November 1785.
30 *LJ*, 26 November 1785.
31 *LJ*, 3, 10, 24 December 1785.
32 *LJ*, 31 December 1785.
33 *LJ*, 24 December 1785, 7, 14 January 1786.
34 *LJ*, 21 January 1786. The line was 'to cross the Loughborough canal or to go to the south of Loughborough'.
35 *LJ*, 21 January, 11 February 1786.
36 *LJ*, 11 February 1786.
37 *LJ*, 8 April 1786.
38 *LJ*, 15 April 1786.
39 *LJ*, 6 May 1786.
40 *LJ*, 5 July 1788.
41 *LJ*, 7 October 1786.
42 *LJ*, 28 October 1786.
43 *LJ*, 11 November 1786.
44 *LJ*, 18 November 1786.
45 *LJ*, 9 December 1786.
46 *LJ*, 27 October 1787.
47 *LJ*, 8 March 1788. The trustees indignantly denied this.
48 *LJ*, 11 October 1788.
49 *LJ*, 6 March 1789.
50 *LJ*, 13 March, 3 April 1789.
51 *LJ*, 15 May 1789.
52 *LJ*, 6 November, 18 December 1789.
53 Public Record Office (British Transport Historical Records LCN 1/1), 12 July 1790. This did not stop the Leicester promoters getting harsh protective clauses in their favour into the Ashby's Act.
54 BTHR LCN 1/1, 28 July 1790.
55 BTHR LCN 1/1, 4 August 1790.
56 Information from Mr P.G. Rattenbury.
57 *LJ*, 31 January 1791.
58 *LJ*, 24 September 1790, 7 January 1791.
59 BTHR LCN 1/1, 22 September 1790.
60 BTHR LCN 1/1, 25 November 1790.

61 BTHR LCN 1/1, 15 January 1791.
62 BTHR LCN 1/1, 24 January 1791.
63 BTHR LCN 1/1, 9 February 1791.
64 BTHR LCN 1/1, 7 January 1791.
65 BTHR LCN 1/1, 26, 28, 30 April 1791.

Chapter 2

1 In 1888 the fall was reported as 8 ft 11½ in and in 1898 as 9 ft 7 in.
2 See above p. 14.
3 For William Fillingham see Peter Stevenson, *The Nutbrook Canal* (1970).
4 See above pp. 15, 17.
5 Information from Mr K.J. Cheetham.
6 *LJ*, 27 July, 14 September 1827.
7 *LJ*, 22 April 1791.
8 *LJ*, 19 May 1791.
9 *LJ*, 24 June 1791.
10 LRO, 3D42/4/2, 5 July 1791.
11 LRO, 3D42/4/2, 1, 15 September 1791.
12 LRO, 3D42/4/2, 1 November 1791.
13 LRO, 3D42/4/2, 20 October, 1 November 1791.
14 LRO, 3D42/4/2, 14 April, 25 May, 2 July 1792.
15 Waterways Museum, Stoke Bruerne.
16 *LH*, 23 June 1792.
17 Stevens, *The Leicester Line*, Chapter 1.
18 Leic. Mus., 3D42/42/2, 29 August 1792.
19 *LJ*, 15 March 1793.
20 LRO Mus., 3D42/4/2, 24 May 1793.
21 *LH*, 6 July 1793.
22 LRO, 3D42/4/2, 4 September 1793.
23 LRO, 3D42/4/2, 11 October, 6 December 1793.
24 LRO, 3D4/2/2, 8 November 1793.
25 *Gentleman's Magazine*, Vol. 63 pt. 2, p. 1144; *LJ*, 20 December 1793.
26 LRO 3D42/4/2, 7 January 1794.
27 LRO 3D42/4/2, 10 January 1794.
28 *LJ*, 10 January 1794; *LH* 11 January 1794. The Leicester and Northamptonshire Union Canal was planned to link the Leicester with a branch of the Grand Junction at Northampton.
29 LRO 3D42/4/2, 27 January 1794.

30 *LH*, 11 January 1794; *LJ*, 31 January 1794.
31 LRO 3D42/4/2, 10 February 1794.
32 *LH*, 22 February 1794; *LJ* 28 February 1794.
33 LRO 3D42/4/2, 28 February 1794; *LJ* 21 March 1794.
34 *LH*, 29 March 1794.
35 *LH*, 19, 24 May, 25 October 1794.
36 LRO, 3D42/4/2, 24 October 1794.
37 *LH*, 1 November 1794.
38 *Gentleman's Magazine*, Vol. 64 pt. 2, p. 1139; *LH*, 1 November 1794; *LJ*, 31 October 1794.

Chapter 3

1 *LH*, 7 November 1794.
2 *LJ*, 12 June 1795.
3 LRO, 3D42/4/2.
4 *LH*, 16 January 1795.
5 *LH*, 13, 27 February 1795.
6 LRO, 3D42/4/2.
7 *LJ*, 1 May 1795.
8 LRO, 3D42/4/2.
9 LRO, 3D42/4/2.
10 LRO, 3D42/4/2.
11 LRO, 3D42/4/2.
12 LRO, 3D42/4/2.
13 LRO, 3D42/4/2.
14 LRO, 3D42/4/2.
15 LRO, 3D42/4/2.
16 LRO, 3D42/4/2.
17 LRO, 3D42/4/2.
18 LRO, 3D42/4/2.
19 *LJ*, 19 May 1797.
20 LRO, 3D42/4/2.
21 *LJ*, 16 February 1798, 21 December 1798.
22 LRO, 3D42/4/2.
23 *LJ*, 21 December 1798.
24 LRO, 3D42/4/2.
25 LRO, 3D42/4/2; *LJ*, 15 June 1798.
26 LRO, 3D42/4/2 (c.f. above, p. 28).
27 *LJ*, 21 September 1798, 7 December 1798.

28 *LJ*, 18 January 1799.
29 *LJ*, 22 February 1799.
30 LRO, 3D42/4/2.
31 LRO, 3D42/4/2.
32 LRO, Herrick MSS 2546.
33 LRO, 3D42/4/2.
34 LRO, 3D42/4/2.
35 *LJ*, 11 April 1800.
36 BTHR LCN 1/17, 7 July 1834.
37 BTHR LCN 1/4, 4 January 1803.
38 BTHR LCN 1/8, 5 August 1804.
39 BTHR LCN 1/4, 15 February 1805.
40 LRO, 3D42/4/2.
41 BTHR LCN 4/4, 13 December 1820.
42 BTHR LCN 1/15, 20 December 1820.

Chapter 4

1 LRO, QS 49/1.
2 BTHR LCN 1/15, 9 September 1814, 24 April 1815.
3 *LJ*, 30 March 1821. In 1821 Stanwick coal was selling at 17s. 6d. (87½p) a ton.
4 *LJ*, 17 May 1833. The average price of Leicestershire coal was 8s. 6d. (42½p) a ton; Whitwick coal fetched 9s. 6d. (47½p).
5 *LC*, 2 March 1839, 6 May 1840.
6 *LJ*, 16 May, 19 December 1834.
7 *LC*, 25 July 1840.
8 BTHR LCN 1/18, 30 June 1841.
9 BTHR LCN 1/19, 1 January 1849.
10 *LJ*, 24 December 1819.
11 *LJ*, 6 September 1816.
12 *LJ*, 22 July 1803.
13 *LJ*, 13 August 1813.
14 *LC*, 26 May 1827.
15 *LC*, 5 April, 5 July, 25 October 1828, 14 March 1829, 9 January 1830, 19 February 1831.
16 *LC*, 30 January, 6 February 1830.
17 LRO, 3D42/4/3.
18 BTHR LCN 1/17, 24 December 1832.
19 BTHR LCN 1/17, 15 May 1834.

20 *LJ*, 24 October 1834.
21 Williams, *The Midland Railway, its Rise and Progress.*
22 BTHR LCN 1/17, 12 April 1833.

Chapter 5

1 Stevens, *The Leicester Line*, pp. 94–5.
2 BTHR LCN 1/20, 27 March 1860.
3 BTHR LCN 1/21, 17 August, 22 October 1869.
4 BTHR LCN 1/22, 5 July 1880.
5 Stocks, *Records of the Borough of Leicester 1603–1688*, p. 539. For the background to Leicester's flood prevention measures, see Rice, *East Midlands Geographer.*
6 *LJ*, 14 February 1873.
7 *LJ*, 29 October 1875.
8 *LJ*, 30 January, 30 April 1880.
9 *LJ*, 23 July, 15 October 1875.
10 *LJ*, 3 May 1878.
11 *LJ*, 8 August 1879.
12 *LJ*, 16 July 1880.
13 *LJ*, 17 September, 8 October 1880.
14 LRO CM 11/1.
15 LRO CM 11/1.
16 BTHR LCN 1/18, 6 January, 26 June, 12 September, 24 September, 9 October 1845.
17 BTHR LCN 1/23, 29 March 1887.
18 BTHR LCN 1/24, 3 December 1896, 5 July 1897.
19 BTHR GJC 1/25, 9 August 1899.
20 BTHR GJC 1/25, 8 November, 13 December 1899.
21 BTHR LCN 1/25, 20 February, 14 March 1901.
22 BTHR LCN 1/25, 8 January 1902.
23 BTHR LCN 1/26, 29 March 1911.
24 BTHR LCN 1/26, 16 November 1911.
25 BTHR LCN 1/27, 2 February 1921.
26 BTHR LCN 1/27, 7 April 1930. The 'old' Grand Union did form part of the 'new' Grand Union, as it had been absorbed by the Grand Junction in 1894, and the Grand Junction was in turn absorbed by the 'new' Grand Union.
27 BTHR LCN 1/27, 21 April 1931.
28 BTHR UCC 1/1, 23 December 1931.

Chapter 6

1 Stevens, *The Leicester Line*, p. 185.
2 Woolfitt, *Idle Women*, p. 202.
3 Ibid., p. 205.
4 *Canals and Inland Waterways: Report of the Board of Survey*: HMSO, 1955.
5 *The Future of the Waterways*: HMSO, 1964.
6 *The Facts about the Waterways*: HMSO, 1965.
7 *Leicester Mercury*, 27 July 1972.
8 J. Priestley, *Historical Account of the Navigable Rivers, Canals, and Railways throughout Great Britain*, 1831.

Chapter 7

1 Information from Mr P. Smythe of Messrs Latham Smythe and New.
2 *LJ*, 22 October 1785.
3 *LJ*, 29 October 1785.
4 *LJ*, 12 November 1785.
5 *LJ*, 10 December 1785.
6 *LJ*, 28 January 1786.
7 *LJ*, 11 February 1786.
8 *LJ*, 15 April 1786.
9 *LJ*, 4 March 1786.
10 *LJ*, 3 June 1786.
11 *LJ*, 31 May 1788.
12 *LJ*, 30 January 1789.
13 *LJ*, 27 February 1789.
14 *LJ*, 3 April 1789.
15 *LJ*, 16 July 1790.
16 *LJ*, 30 July, 6 August 1790.
17 *LJ*, 29 April 1791.
18 BTHR LCN 1/1, 9 February 1791 and Chapter 1, p. 17.
19 *LJ*, 11 July 1794.
20 *LJ*, 28 September 1792, 11 July 1794.
21 *LH*, 3 April 1795.
22 *LJ*, 22 June 1804.
23 *LJ*, 16 January 1795.
24 *LJ*, 20 December 1793.
25 *LJ*, 10 January 1794. The villages of the Wreake Valley, especially

its lower part, stand well away from the river on account of flood danger, and the side cut and basin known as Rearsby wharf was midway between the villages of Rearsby and Ratcliffe.

26 *LJ*, 31 October 1794.
27 *LH*, 2 January 1795.
28 *LH*, 3 April 1795.
29 *LJ*, 19 June 1795.
30 *LJ*, 29 November 1795.
31 *LJ*, 13 June 1800.
32 *LJ*, 3 April 1801.
33 *LJ*, 30 March 1804.
34 *LJ*, 22 June 1804.
35 *LJ*, 14 August 1807.
36 *LJ*, 6 February 1819.
37 Drury Lowe Papers Dr E. 134, Nottingham University; information from Mr P. Stevenson.
38 LRO, 3D42/4/2.
39 BTHR LCN 1/1,
40 LRO, 3D42/4/2.
41 LRO, 3D42/4/3.
42 BTHR LCN 1/18, 5 July 1841, 12 January 1842.
43 LRO, 3D42/4/23/8.
44 Stevens, 'The Midland Railway's Syston and Peterborough Branch, 1845–8' *Journal of the Railway and Canal Historical Society*, Vol. XIX, No. 1, 1973.
45 House of Lords Record Office: MS Evidence on the S and P Rly Bill, 1845; Minutes of Evidence to the Select Committee on Railways and Canals Amalgamations, 1846; Minutes of Evidence, Commons Committee of S and P Rly Bill, 1846.
46 Drury Lowe Papers Dr E. 134, Nottingham University; information from Mr P. Stevenson.
47 BTHR LCN 1/19, 18 October, 29 November 1849.
48 BTHR LCN 1/19, 1 July, 27 December 1849, 1 July 1850, 7 October 1852.
49 BTHR LCN 1/19.
50 BTHR PYB, 1/568.
51 *LC*, 14 July 1876.
52 *LJ*, 9 February 1877.
53 *LJ*, 4 May 1877.
54 *LJ*, 11 May 1827.

55 *LJ*, 24 August 1877.
56 *LJ*, 15 March 1878.
57 *LJ*, 26 July 1878.
58 *LJ*, 17 June 1881.
59 *LJ*, 1 November 1878.

Bibliography

Hadfield, Charles, *The Canals of the East Midlands*. Newton Abbot, David & Charles, second edition, 1970.

Patterson, A. Temple, 'The Making of the Leicestershire Canals', *Transactions of the Leicestershire Archaeological Society*, XXVII. The Guildhall, Leicester, 1951.

Priestley, J., *Historical Account of the Navigable Rivers, Canals, and Railways throughout Great Britain*. 1831.

Rolt, L.T.C., *Narrow Boat*. London, Eyre & Spottiswood, 1944.

Sallis, R.H. de, *Bradshaw's Canals and Navigable Rivers of England and Wales*. Newton Abbot, David & Charles, 1904, reprinted 1969.

Tew, D.H., *The Oakham Canal*. Wymondham, Rutland, Brewhouse Press, 1968.

Woolfitt, S., *Idle Women*. London, Ernest Benn Ltd, 1947.

Index